Samuel Richardson as Anonymous Editor and Printer

Samuel Richardson as Anonymous Editor and Printer

Recycling Texts for the Book Market

John A. Dussinger

ANTHEM PRESS

Anthem Press
An imprint of Wimbledon Publishing Company
www.anthempress.com

This edition first published in UK and USA 2024
by ANTHEM PRESS
75–76 Blackfriars Road, London SE1 8HA, UK
or PO Box 9779, London SW19 7ZG, UK
and
244 Madison Ave #116, New York, NY 10016, USA

© 2024 John A. Dussinger

The author asserts the moral right to be identified as the author of this work.

All rights reserved. Without limiting the rights under copyright reserved above,
no part of this publication may be reproduced, stored or introduced into
a retrieval system, or transmitted, in any form or by any means
(electronic, mechanical, photocopying, recording or otherwise),
without the prior written permission of both the copyright
owner and the above publisher of this book.

British Library Cataloguing-in-Publication Data
A catalogue record for this book is available from the British Library.

Library of Congress Cataloging-in-Publication Data: 2023947910
A catalog record for this book has been requested.

ISBN-13: 978-1-78527-353-7 (Hbk)
ISBN-10: 1-78527-353-1 (Hbk)

Cover Credit: Woodcut of early printing workshop (Public Domain)

This title is also available as an e-book.

CONTENTS

1. Introduction to *The True Briton*: Oaths of Allegiance and Women's Empowerment   1
2. Selected Texts of *The True Briton*   7
3. Introduction to *The Weekly Miscellany*: Sarah Chapone, Women's "Championess"   29
4. Selected Texts of *The Weekly Miscellany*   47

Conclusion: Richardson's Press and Women's Entry into Public Life   129

Bibliography   133

Index   139

Chapter 1

INTRODUCTION TO *THE TRUE BRITON*: OATHS OF ALLEGIANCE AND WOMEN'S EMPOWERMENT

During the first two decades of his printing career, Richardson was associated with seven journals: *The True Briton* (1723–1724), *The Plain Dealer* (1724–1725), *The Daily Journal* (1721–1737), *The Prompter* (1734–1736), *The Daily Gazetteer* (1735–1746), *The Weekly Miscellany* (1733–36), and *The Citizen* (1739). Years before the appearance of his first work of fiction, he was already known among his fellow printers for being a gifted writer. In the January 1736 issue of the *Gentleman's Magazine* (p. 51), Edward Cave, the editor, observed that Richardson had "often agreeably entertain'd with Elegant Disquisitions in Prose." Among these anonymous works were likely pieces contributed to some of these journals as well as such pamphlets as *The Infidel Convicted* (1731), *The Oxford Methodists* (1733), *The Apprentice's Vade Mecum* (1734), and the *Seasonable Examination of the Pleas and Pretensions of the Proprietors of, and Subscribers to, Play-Houses, Erected in Defiance of the Royal License* (1735).

Since anonymous publication in this period was a closely guarded secret between writers and printers, the inquisitive reader today has few opportunities to establish authorship beyond a reasonable doubt. The only recorded attribution by early commentators to identify Richardson's anonymous contributions, one to the *True Briton*, is found in John Nichols's *Literary Anecdotes*, where in a footnote he states that "it seems highly probable that the sixth [No. 6 (June 21, 1723)] was written by himself as it is much in his manner." Although earlier Richardson scholars have dismissed this attribution, after a more thorough examination of this journal, I found grounds for suspecting that this and at least 11 other issues owe something to this printer. In any case, the political themes in letters signed *A.B.* in *True Briton* No. 9 (July 1, 1713); No. 19 (August 19, 1723); No. 24 (August 23, 1723); and No. 25 (August 26, 1723) are closely connected and appear to be written by the same person.[1] As

---

1 See my article, "Samuel Richardson's 'Elegant Disquisitions': Anonymous Writing in the *True Briton* and Other Journals?" *Studies in Bibliography*, Vol. 53 (2000), pp. 195–226.

I will argue, the five letters in this journal signed with women's names also appear to be written by the same person, and most likely Richardson.

Two major crises influenced Richardson's first years as printer: the South Sea Bubble of 1720 and the Jacobite Rebellion of 1721–1722, associated with the Bishop of Rochester, Francis Atterbury. Both of these crises contributed to Robert Walpole's rise to power, and his repressive policies led to a vigorous opposition. The Duke of Wharton's journal, *The True Briton*, printed in its entirety by Richardson (from June 3, 1723, to February 17, 1724), was sharply critical of Walpole and thus a frequent target of government censors. Consequently, in his very first years as an independent printer, Richardson already showed his agility in avoiding arrest for subversive publications.[2] But Richardson began life as an outlier who felt alien toward the Hanoverian politics of his time and seems to have imagined what Freud termed the "family romance" to compensate his sense of loss accordingly. His reference to the father of his patron, Thomas, first Marquess of Wharton, in *Clarissa*, third ed. (1751), 2: 19, reveals his life-long interest in this family. Since Philip himself claimed to be following in his father's footsteps as an "Old Whig" as opposed to the corrupt makeover under Walpole, we may assume that "true Briton" was a code word for "true Whig."

In his remarkable letter to his Dutch translator, Johannes Stinstra, the only autobiographical account that we have, Richardson claimed that his father's known sympathies with the Duke of Monmouth and the first Earl of Shaftesbury prompted his removal from the City at the time of Monmouth's execution in 1685. This explanation, however, is mysterious since records indicate that his father stayed in London some three years after this direful event.[3] What really matters, however, is that Richardson adopted this story as if to underscore a father as a victim of a lost cause. Monmouth was executed for treason on July 15, 1685. Many of his supporters were tried during the "Bloody Assizes," led by Judge Jeffreys, and were condemned to death or transportation. James II was then able to consolidate his power and reigned until 1688, when he was overthrown in a *coup d'état* by William of Orange

---

2 Keith Maslen, *Samuel Richardson of London Printer* (Dunedin: University of Otago Press, 2001), pp. 27–28. *Daily Journal*, No. 1038 (May 19, 1724): "Mr. Nathaniel Mist, for libelling [sic] the Government in his *Weekly Journal* of June 8, 1723, to pay a Fine of 100 l. to suffer a Years Imprisonment, and to find Sureties for his good Behaviour during Life.

Mr. Thomas Payne, convicted on four several Informations, for a late Paper, call'd, *The True Briton*, was fined 400 l. that is to say, 100 l. for each Libel, to suffer a Years Imprisonment, and to find Sureties for hs good Behaviour during Life."

3 *The Richardson-Stinstra Correspondence and Stinstra's Prefaces to* CLARISSA, ed. William C. Slattery (Carbondale and Edwardsville: Southern Illinois University Press, 1969).

in the "Glorious Revolution." In 1723, Richardson may have seen a parallel between the current government backlash against Bishop Francis Atterbury and all suspected Jacobites, on the one hand, and the victims of the "Bloody Assizes," on the other. The references to the unjust punishment of the South Sea directors may imply yet another parallel to the victims of the Atterbury scandal.

Richardson's printing of *True Briton* reveals, I would argue, his political sympathies already at the beginning of his printing career. As a flamboyant Tory dissident who openly courted the support of the City leaders and tradesmen, while starting up his satirical journal, the Duke of Wharton apparently turned to Richardson as his printer for some reason, and it may be that he already recognized his talent as a writer with strong Non-juror sentiments. Unfortunately, Richardson's correspondence with Wharton no longer exists, but evidently there was more than a strictly business relationship between them. This mercurial and self-destructive aristocrat has long been regarded as an inspiration for the character of Robert Lovelace, and it would not be surprising if Richardson could respect his literary ability while deploring his moral failings.

In any case, it appears that Richardson took a more than business interest as the printer of this journal; looking ahead to his emergence as the foremost novelist of the period, it is important to see how the various letters to the editor of this journal supposedly written by women were likely his own contributions. Five issues with letters to the editor signed with women's names appear to reveal Richardson's hand: *True Briton* No. 28 (September 6, 1723) and No. 34 (September 27, 1723), signed *Athalia Dormant*; 45 (November 4, 1723), signed *Conscientia*; No. 47 (11 November 1723), signed *Misericordia*; and No. 71 (February 3, 1723–1724), signed *Violette*. A fifth issue with an impersonation, an ironic response to these women's complaints, No. 61 (December 30, 1723), signed *Old Batchelor*, is stylistically similar and probably by Richardson. Finally, *True Briton* No. 66 (January 17, 1723–1724), a digest of Plutarch's *Political Precepts*, signed *S.R.*, may be the earliest example of this printer's work in making abridgements and indexes, and even openly acknowledged here.

What seems especially close to self-revelation is that both letters signed "*Athalia Dormant*" directly refer to the "woful Experience" of the printer while marketing a controversial political journal when the Walpole government was exerting all of its legal power to repress dissent. In *True Briton* No. 28, *Athalia* speaks ironically on behalf of the printer against introducing religious texts to edify atheist readers, who are presumably inclined to support Walpole in the repression of High Church Tory opponents. Perhaps, in light of how women were now engaged in public demonstrations against the government, having a woman's voice here is merely giving credit to their political activism at the time. But the sardonic argument here anticipates the similar strategy of *Belinda*'s in warning William Webster, editor of *The Weekly Miscellany*, against printing feminist material for fear of losing readership. As a printer and sometime bookseller, Richardson was always concerned with the problem of gaining a profitable circulation for his publications. In the second letter by *Athalia*, the satire is against even allowing opposition journalists to hack the space in *True Briton* columns for writing too dull to attract any readers at all. Presumably, even though hired vendors are sent to the coffee houses to make a point of asking for this particular paper as a strategy for increasing circulation, they themselves are too ashamed to carry out their task, knowing the poor quality of those contributors to the *True Briton*.

In *True Briton* No. 71, *Violette*'s attack on masquerades reflects a life-long obsession with Richardson, who addresses the problem in all three of his novels as a dangerous trap for women. This particular letter was probably in reference to a recent event reported in the *Daily Journal* No. 928 (January 11, 1723–4) and printed by Richardson: an article about a large masquerade ball where the king and the prince attended in costume. The next issue, No. 929 (January 13, 1723–1724), reports that "On Friday last a Person of Note turn'd his youngest Daughter out of Doors for her Disobedience, in going to the Masquerade, contrary to his Commands." Then, No. 946 (February 1, 1723–1724) reports wryly:

> We are inform'd, that at the last Ball or Masquerade a Person came amongst the Assembly habited like a News Cryer or Hawker, with several Pamphlets under one of his Arms, crying, *The Lord Bishop of London's Sermon against the Masquerades;* whether by way of Ridicule or Admonition we cannot take upon us to say; but however the Company obliged the Person to leave the House.

Even though Richardson himself may not have had a role in writing these newspaper articles, as a printer, he doubtless read them before creating *Violette*'s moral condemnation of masquerades.

On January 6, 1723, Edmund Gibson, the Lord Bishop of London, preached a sermon to the Societies for the Reformation of Manners at St. Mary-le-Bow against the prevailing "Vice and Profaneness" and the "various Engines contriv'd by a corrupt Generation, to support them" (p. 19). He fulminates in particular against masquerades, "as they deprive Virtue and Religion of their last Refuge, I mean *Shame*; which keeps multitudes of Sinners within the bounds of *Decency*, after they have broken thro' all the Ties of Principle and Conscience" (p. 19). At the end of his harangue, Gibson invokes xenophobia by referring to the ambassador from Louis XIV's court who introduced this "Engine" as a means "to *Enslave* us; and indeed there is not a more effectual way to enslave a People, than first to dispirit and enfeeble them by Licentiousness and Effeminacy" (p. 20). His pronouncement that "this is a Diversion that no *true Englishman* ought to be fond of" may also be an implicit criticism of the German king and prince who appeared in costume at that event. But despite Gibson's condemnation, the masquerade was to flourish all the more with the opening of such pleasure gardens as Vauxhall and Ranelagh in the next decades.

By contrast to Gibson, however, Richardson's female critic is mostly concerned with the exposure of naïve young women once they drop their guard while indulging in the uninhibited play of masquerade balls:

> THE Freedoms of a *Masquerade* are but very indifferent Methods of initiating fine young Ladies into Conversation, when they have taken Leave of their Governesses, and find themselves freed from those strict Rules of Virtue and Morality, which are too apt to sit uneasy on the Gay and the Youthful Part of the Sex, which therefore is more susceptible of Impressions of a contrary Nature. Thus prepar'd, and falling into the Ribaldries of a *Masquerade,* what Improvement may not be expected from the Minds of ductile Youth? *Excessive Liberties* naturally bring on *Excessive Restraints*: and 'twill be found proper in Time, perhaps, to immure the Sex as in *Turkey,* and other Parts, to confine those Bodies, whose Minds are too apt to be gadding after such enormous Diversions.

As a lifelong avid promoter of matrimony, Richardson especially deplores the consequences of indiscreet women losing their reputation and hence their chances to find good and honest husbands on the marriage market. First and foremost was the dire necessity of preserving women to be eligible wives to maintain marriages as the mainstay of stable families.

Even if Richardson was personally inclined to defend women's freedom of conscience beforehand, Wharton's periodical itself thrust him into the whole female activism during the Atterbury crisis, when in 1723 the government demanded oaths of allegiance from women for the first and only time in the history of allegiance oaths.[4] Ironically, the government's sweeping mandate actually empowered women all the more by giving them the status of being eligible on principle to take oaths. Whether he actually wrote the letter, he at least printed it and could scarcely oppose the views of *A.Z.* in *True Briton*

---

4 Edward Vallance, "Women, Politics and the 1723 Oaths of Allegiance to George I," *The Historical Journal,* Vol. 29, No. 4 (2016), pp. 975–999.

No. 21 (August 12, 1723), "The Humble Petition of all the Rich Unmarry'd Women of Great Britain," protesting the Oaths of Allegiance on the grounds that women are not allowed a role in parliament. *Conscientia* in *True Briton* No. 45 (November 24, 1723) pleads against the mandate on the principle that they must first know exactly what they are being asked to swear to before committing themselves. By contrast, a satiric letter signed "Old Batchelor" in *True Briton* No. 61 (December 30, 1723) goes even a step further by requiring women to take an oath of allegiance to their husbands as a condition of entering marriage.

Chapter 2

SELECTED TEXTS OF
THE TRUE BRITON

1. ***The True Briton.*** **No. 21. Monday, August 12. 1723. [*A. Z.*]**

Vol. 1, pp. 178–185.

THE great Care which the Parliament hath taken for the Publick Welfare, is evident thro' the whole Course of their Proceedings; but their [*sic*] is no greater instance of their Zeal, than the Act which pass'd the last Sessions to oblige the Female Part of this Kingdom to take the Oaths.

OUR wise Administration justly call'd to mind the fatal instance of a certain Island, where the Women murder'd the Men,[1] and therefore, thought it prudent and necessary, for the security of our happy Establishment, to oblige them to take those Oaths which are the Bulwarks of the Protestant Succession.

THERE is another Reason which might be of some Weight on this Occasion; which is, That many Great Men[2] are influenc'd by the Ladies in all Matters whatsoever, and therefore, it is certainly most proper to try their Loyalty in the strictest Manner we can.

I COULD have wish'd the little *Ebony Doctor*[3] would have thought proper to imploy his Pen at this Juncture, to shew the *Nature of Oaths*; for the Ladies, I

---

1 Reference to the women on the island of Lemnos who massacred their husbands after being rejected by them in favor of slaves. See Marius D'Assigny, *The Poetical History: Being a Compleat Collection of all the Stories Necessary for a Perfect Understanding of the Greek and Latin Poets, and other Ancient Authors. Written Originally in French by the Learned Jesuit P. Galtruchius*, 8th ed. (London, 1701), p. 234.
2 Allusion to Robert Walpole, the unscrupulous Whig leader of Parliament, the first "Prime Minister," who enhanced his power by exploiting the hysteria over Jacobite plots. See Edward Pearce, *The Great Man: Sir Robert Walpole: Scoundrel, Genius and Britain's First Prime Minister* (London: Random House, 2007).
3 White Kennett (1660–1728), Bishop of Peterborough. Although Kennett opposed the ecclesiastical policy of James II and preached against "popery," he rejected the

fear, will generally take them without understanding any of them, except the *Abjuration,* which is conceived in plain and easy Terms. I dare say the Bishops will supply his Defect, and will not decline giving any scrupulous Conscience all possible Satisfaction.

IT is said, That since the supposed Riot at *Cripplegate* a certain *Eminent* and *Honest* Lawyer has represented to his Friends, that it would be proper this Law should be extended to the Women; and that it should be Felony for Twelve Females to meet together, and not disperse on the Reading of the Proclamation; but it is hoped, that a certain Lady not far from St. *James*'s will have Interest enough to prevent this Attempt, which would intirely destroy her Assemblée.[4]

WHATEVER secret Methods the Ladies have of concealing their Sex, and creeping into Power, are unknown; yet it is certain, That there has scarce been an Age formerly, but Old Women have sate in the Cabinet, as M — rs[5]; in *Westminster-Hall as* J—es,[6] and in the H—se of L—ds as B—ps.[7] **[180]** The Little *Ebony Doctor* at present bears that Character among the rational Part of Mankind.

IT is to be hop'd such a Number of Persons will conform on this Occasion, as will convince all *Europe,* That any Attempts to disturb us are vain; and the Ladies Zeal at this Juncture, will, in some Measure, atone for the Death of Cardinal *Du Bois.*[8]

FOR fear they should grow familiar with Swearing, and not distinguish between a Legal and Illegal Oath, it is said, the Third Commandment will

---

"Declaration for Liberty of Conscience" in 1688. Subsequently, however, he supported the revolution and whig cause against Atterbury and his high church circle. After a shooting accident injured his skull he wore a large velvet black patch on his forehead and hence the nickname of "Ebony Doctor."

4 Satiric mimicry of the 1715 Riot Act, which gave local authorities the right to order the dispersal of any gathering of more than twelve people who were "unlawfully, riotously, and tumultuously assembled together." During the 1720s the *Beau Monde* had begun to hold large parties in their homes that offered opportunities for women to sample the marriage market. Later in the century public buildings like Almack's or the Assembly Rooms at Bath were instituted to accommodate larger numbers for conversation between the sexes.

5 "Ministers."
6 "Judges."
7 "House of Lords as Bishops."
8 Guillaume Dubois (1656-1723) was a powerful French cardinal and statesman under Louis XIV.

be speedily printed, and given *Gratis* to all those Women that shall not refuse to comply with the Pleasure of the Parliament.⁹

I AM very much oblig'd to my worthy Friend A. Z, for his Letter, and hope I shall hear more frequently from him.

To the True Briton.
*Egregiam vero lauden, et spolia ampla refertis
   Tuque puerque tuus* ----------¹⁰

SIR,

I AM assured that I recommend my self to you, when I confess that I am a *Zealous Whig*; and to keep up my Character of being *Staunch*, I have always thought myself under an Obligation to defend the Actions of my Masters: And though this Principle may have sometimes involved me in seeming Contradictions, yet I never flinched. Accordingly, in the late Queen's Time,¹¹ I roar'd out for the noble Liberty **[p. 181]** of *Resistance*; and since her Decease, for the noble Liberty of *blind Obedience*;¹² In 1719. [*sic*] I congratulated the Nation upon its Prospect of being freed from its Debts by the Wise *South-Sea Scheme*; And in 1720, I railed at the Directors, and swore they were all *Jacobites*:¹³ At the Beginning of King GEORGE's Reign, I cursed the late Lord *Bol---e*, and the *Lord Har—t* for being *Peace-*Makers¹⁴; and am now perfectly fond of them for being *Plot-Demolishers*. But above all, I have been remarkably loud in the Defence of the Proceedings in Parliament, because I look upon That as the Quintessence of my Party; and because no one durst contradict me; for you must know, I have always been thought an *Informer*.¹⁵ Thus have

---

9 Third commandment is against taking the name of God in vain, i.e., *swearing* in vain.
10 "You are rich with splendid praise, and ample spoil You and your boy." Virgil's *Aeneid*, Book IV, 93–94.
11 Queen Anne (1665-1714).
12 "[...] a TORY, one who is for *Passive Obedience* and *Non Resistance* to the Will of the Prince, for the *Hereditary Succession* of the Crown without any limitations, yielding a servile and blind obedience to the Prerogative," John Toland, *The Memorial of the State if England, in Vindication of the Queen, the Church, and the Administration* (London, 1705), p. 77.
13 South Sea Bubble of 1720.
14 "Bolingbroke" and "Harley," "t" apparently wrong terminal alphabet letter for name "Harley."
15 A government spy. "[...] a Common Informer and Prosecutor ought to be treated as a Branch of Legislative Authority," Humphrey Mackworth, *A Vindication of the Rights of the Commons of England* (London, 1701), p. 31.

I behaved my-self Seven Years,[16] and did design the same for Seven-times Seven; But, alas! I find my Resolution begins to stagger at a Bill passed in the last Sessions; by which all the Fair Ladies in Great Britain, that have any Fortunes, and no Husbands, are obliged before the 25th of December next, to take Three stout Oaths of *Allegiance, Supremacy,* and *Abjuration*; which Three Words are enough to frighten half the Female World.[17]

I HAVE puzzled myself in vain, to find out what the Ladies have done to draw down the Fury of the Parliament upon them. I once thought the Lord *Nithsdale's* escaping in Womens Cloaths,[18] might cause this *Whig-Aversion* to *Petticoats*; but that is too long ago. Then I recollected, that several of that Sex waited on Bishop *Atterbury*,[19] to take Leave of Him before He embarked; but this is too late, for the *Swearing Bill* passed before he went: Besides, it is very well known, They were more concerned for his **[p. 182]** *Person* than *Principles*, unjustly fearing the King would not find out as *Handsome* a Man to succeed Him.

I AM at a Loss to understand the *Policy* of this Act; which will certainly exasperate the Sufferers by it against the Government; and, without doubt, a *Gracious King* and a *Fine Gentleman* would be, at least, as desirous of the Affections of his *Female* Subjects as of his *Male*: Besides, the Number of *Non-jurors* is so very small, that it was impossible to make them considerable without helping them to so great a Reinforcement of *Non-juresses* as they will now have.

---

16 Reference to Jacobite Plot of 1715.
17 "The Oaths Act required both men and women over the age of eighteen to take the oaths of allegiance, supremacy, and abjuration before 25 December 1723 or register their names and property in court. Failure either to subscribe or to register would result in the forfeiture of an individual's estate." Vallance, "Women, Politics and the 1723 Oaths of Allegiance to George I," p. 979.

Cf. Richardson's long footnote to *Clarissa*: "See *Numb.* xxx. Where it is declared, whose vows shall be binding, and whose not. The vows of a Man, or of a Widow, are there pronounced to be indispensable; because they are Sole, and subject to no other domestic authority. But the vows of a Single woman, and of a Wife, if the Father of the one, or the Husband of the other, disallow of them as soon as they know them, are to be of no force. A matter highly necessary to be known; by all young Ladies especially, whose designing addressers too often endeavour to engage them by vows; and then plead Conscience and Honour to them to hold them down to the performance." Richardson then quotes Numbers xxx, verses 3-5, & 16. *Clarissa*, 1st ed. (1748), Vol. 2, p.289.
18 William Maxwell, 5th Earl of Nithsdale (1676–1744), escaped execution by exchanging clothes with his wife's maid.
19 Francis Atterbury (1663–1732). High Church clergyman, Tory, and Jacobite. *ODNB*.

IT is very amazing, that among so many amorous, so many pretty well dressed Noblemen and Gentlemen, the Ladies should not have a Party strong enough to support their Interest; nay, not so much as a *Protest* enter'd in Favour of them against a Bill, which must necessarily cause more Talk, and more ill will than the Famous *Quarantine Act*.[20]

UPON farther Thoughts, I am apt to imagine, that the Reason of these Proceedings may be accounted for from the great Hurry of Employ our Representatives have been in about Dr. *Atterbury* and *Kelly*,[21] &c. Zeal for the Hanover Succession has made them unattentive to the Secret Whisperings of *Nature*, which every Man of good Sense and good Nature is known to carry about him in Favour of this Beautiful Part of the Creation. But let the Ladies know for their Comfort, that the General Council of *Great Britain* does not think itself Infallible in its Determinations; but has been known to have repeal'd an Act, **[p. 183]** almost as soon as it was made, and before it was put in Execution.

IN Confidence of this, I have drawn up the Form of a Petition to the House of Commons to redress this real Grievance: I desire it may be left with the Printer of this Paper, for the Ladies to subscribe: which I am persuaded, they will do; and that they will flock to the Parliament-House with as great Unanimity as the Roman Matrons did to the Senate, when they apprehended a Law was enacting to allow each Senator Two Wives.[22]

---

20 "The Quarantine Act 1721 was a health protection measure passed by the Parliament of Great Britain. During the 18th century, the age of empire and sailing ships in England, outbreaks of diseases such as the plague seemed to travel from country to country very rapidly. Parliament responded to this threat by establishing the Quarantine Act in 1721(8 Geo c 10)." *Wikipedia.*
21 George Kelley (*c.*1680–1762), one of the Jacobite conspirators.
22 The story of Papirius's fabrication to his mother about the Roman senators being allowed two wives appears in Aulus Gellius, *The Attic Nights,* translated by W. Beloe, 3 Vols. (London, 1795), Vol. 1, pp. 86–88; and in Ambrosius Aurelius Theodosius Macrobius, *Saturnalia,* 6.19–26, Loeb Classical Library (Cambridge: Harvard University Press, 2011), Vol. 1, pp. 60–63. The tale is also recounted in the anonymous medieval *Gesta Romanorum* and in Hartmann Schedel's *Liber Chronicarum* (Nuremberg, 1493). My thanks to Terry L. Meyers of William and Mary for his e-mail tip to a Google source for this information. It seems doubtful that many of the readers of this journal would recognize this allusion to Papirius, but it attests to Wharton's literary acuteness and quickness in Latin. This same allusion, however, appears in *The Weekly Miscellany,* No. 300 (October 23, 1736). Perhaps Richardson kept a commonplace book for such gems.

To the Honourable House of Commons,
In PARLIAMENT Assembled,
The Humble Petition of all the Rich Unmarry'd Women of *Great-Britain*;

Sheweth,

THAT Your Petitioners are in the utmost Consternation to hear that an Act passed in the last Session to oblige Your Petitioners to so unusual a thing as Swearing. We are not sensible, that we have been guilty of any Actions or Expressions that can bring us under a Suspicion of Disloyalty to the Government. We have rais'd and lower'd our Heads, have inlarg'd or contracted our Hoops, have shew'd our Best Cloaths and Airs on Birth-Nights and in Drawing-Rooms, in strict Conformity to the present Establishment. We have prefer'd the Love of our Country to that of Fine Cloaths; and, in Obedience to **[p. 184]** Parliament, have made up our India Damasks and Chinces into Curtains, Quilts and Toylettes, not daring to use 'em even for Under-Petticoats. We have besides been so busy of late in adjusting the Cut of the Sleeve, and other Affairs of great Consequence, that we have had very little Time to inquire into the Pope's Authority, or the Distinctions of Indefeasible Hereditary and Parliamentary Right.

WE are also humbly of Opinion, That it is not agreeable to Equity to load us with Double Taxes for Disaffection, since Loyalty does not qualify us for the Profits of State Offices. If therefore, this Act must continue in Force, we humbly expect to be impower'd by another to send an equal Number of Parliament-Women to the House; That one of the Secretaries of State may be of our Sex; and, That we may have the prodigious Pleasure of being admitted into the Secrets of the Privy-Council. Neither can we conceive what Prejudice it could be to the Government, if, in the Time of Peace, we should come in for a Share of the Posts in the Army.

WE also beg Leave to remind Your Honours, That many Members of this House have often been Petitioners to Us; have flung themselves at our Feet; and with Oaths and Protestations, have owned, how ready they were to dye for us; and what Power we have over them. We shall therefore have Reason to doubt of the Sincerity of these Expressions, if we cannot succeed in this so reasonable a Request; or, if we have that extensive Power, we may be provok'd to exert it.

IF this Act is calculated with Design to force us to put our Persons and Fortunes into the Hands of **[p. 185]** *Men that will Swear, we are resolved to pluck up our spirit, and to sacrifice Part of our Riches to our Resentment; And we take this Opportunity of letting the House know our Resolutions, That, unless this Clause be immediately repealed, those Members who are unmarry'd, shall continue so; and those that have Wives, may, perhaps, hear of this, when they would chuse to be asleep.*

AFTER ALL, We dare assure Ourselves, That we shall have our Tender Consciences indulged as far the Quakers were, not long since;[23] *and, That, if we must give the Government any Security for our Affections, it may be by our usual Way of Protesting and Vowing. In a Word, Do any thing to free us from Swearing;*
And Your Petitioners will ever Pray, &c.

THESE Arguments, assisted by the Moving Eloquence of so many Beautiful Faces, will, I doubt not, prevail: But if not, I hope the P---- y-C----cil[24] will send out Injunctions to the Bishops and Ministers of every Diocess and Parish, to instruct our Weak Sisters in *Casuistry*; to teach them to confute *Bellarmine*;[25] and to inform Them of the Extent of *Faithful* and *True Allegiance*; and whether or no They are obliged by it to wear Swords, and ride astride.[26]

I am, SIR,
Your Humble Servant,
A. Z.

2. The True Briton. No. 28. Friday, September 6. 1723. [*Athalia Dormant*]

Vol. I, p. 243.

To the Author of the TRUE BRITON.

Dear SIR,

A Current Report has been propagated at all the Tea-Tables in Town, that you intend to Print the *Ten Commandments* and the *Lord's Prayer*, in your *True Briton*, for the Information and Edification of certain People, who are

---

23 Quaker Act of 1721, which allowed these dissenters to forego taking oaths of allegiance on grounds of their religious beliefs. Speaker of the House Arthur Onslow, Richardson's dear friend, supported this Act. But the Duke of Wharton spoke against it by way of improving his reputation as a defender of the Established Church. See *The Historical Register, Volume VI. For the Year 1721* (London, 1721).
24 "Privy Council."
25 Bellarmine: Robert Bellarmine (Italian: *Roberto Francesco Romolo Bellarmino*; 4 October 1542–17 September 1621) "From his research grew *Disputationes de controversiis christianae fidei* (also called *Controversiae*), first published at Ingolstadt in 1581–1593. This major work was the earliest attempt to systematize the various religious disputes between Catholics and Protestants." *Wikipedia*.
26 At this time women were expected to ride horses side-saddle. But with this revolutionary empowerment they ride henceforth like men with legs stretched on each side of the saddle.

supposed never to have heard of such things. Now, Sir, I, in the Name of many of your Female Admirers, earnestly beg of you as you would avoid utter Demolition, to desist from such a bold Enterprize, 'till you have consulted the several Orders of Men in this Kingdom, whether the Times will bear so Critical a Publication. For you must needs know, by the woful Experience[27] of your Printer, what Misconstructions every thing is liable to that that [sic] you publish, since whatever would be styl'd a Panegyrick in other Papers, has been generally deemed a Reflection in yours. And besides, the very inserting of 'em in the *True Briton*, will be sufficient to make all the *Modern Whigs* in the Kingdom expunge them from their Bibles, and remove them as far from their *Sight*, as they have long been from their *Hearts* and *Practices*.

Your Zealous Admirer,
Athaliah Dormant.

3. The True Briton. No. 34. Friday, September 27. 1723. [Athalia Dormant]

Vol. I, 291–294

We shall give the following Letter a Place in this Paper, and, provided our Fair Correspondent keeps the Conditions she prescribes to herself for the future, shall not scruple to acknowledge the Favour of her Letters: But *Conciseness* is what must be insisted on, because of the *Wretchedness* of the Subject wherewith she proposes to *sully* her fair Fingers.[28]

To the Author of the TRUE BRITON.
Dear SIR],
I THINK the Method you take of despising your stupid Adversaries, is intirely worthy of the *True Briton:* But yet I cannot forbear having some Compassion[29] for the poor Creatures, to see how *dully* **[292]** they labour to merit your Notice, and beg the *Means* of *Life* at your Hands. I am told by one of my Admirers, That those few Coffee-Houses, where the Beneficence of

---

27 "woful experience" – 1/2 in *ECF.*

****

28 If Wharton was the editor of this issue, it would not be surprising to find his advising Richardson as possible contributor of this letter against wordiness—a problem that this author himself acknowledged throughout his career as writer.

29 "She Seemed, as I thought, to be Moved to Some Compassion," *Pamela, or Virtue Rewarded*, 1st ed., 2 Vols. (1741), Vol. 1, p. 218.

their Paymasters encourages people to take in their Papers, are quite ty'rd out with the Daily Complaints made of them; and that the very Persons who are *hir'd* to inquire for them in Publick, in order to make 'em noted, are asham'd to ask for 'em, lest all the Gentlemen round should judge of their *Intellects* by the *Choice* of their *Papers*.

This, good Sir, is certainly enough to exasperate against you Persons of more Wit, and less Temper than your Antagonists seem to be. They repine in Secret, I am told, at your Neglect of 'em: And t'other Day, in a *dark Corner* of a certain Coffee-Room near St. *James's*,[30] the motly [*sic*] Crew of *Sycophants* and *Blunderers*[31] got together, and were over-heard to mutter out their Discontents and Despair.

AN abandon'd Wretch, who bears in his very Face the Stamp of Villain and Apostate, and seems peculiarly branded as well by the transcendant [*sic*][32] Ugliness of his Person, as the still more hideous Deformity of his Mind,[33] which has long display'd itself in ridiculing every thing *Divine* and *Humane*, began the Condoleance [*sic*] with his Fellow-Labourers *Ams-Ace* the expell'd *Poetaster*, and *Stupid* the *Publican*, who were accompany'd with their good Ally and Confederate *Pam'*, a late exploded *Prologue-monger*, and several *Eves-droppers* and *Informers*, who make up this *diminutive* Cabal. In Bitterness of Heart he curst your Contempt of their Papers, and declared, that their *Grand Patron* was determin'd to withdraw their Salaries, **[293]** if they could shew no greater Merit than they had hitherto done for continuing them.

THEN frightfully grinning, with violent Execrations, he vociferated, Is there such a Difference between Men and Men, that I who have endeavour'd to confound all Orders and Distinctions in the World, and have my Itinerant Name on Record in all Places necessary to preserve its villainous Existence, should not be able to provoke this d----n'd Author to take the least Notice of us. Our Business would be done if he would but once name us in his accursed Papers. But (continued he with his usual Imprecations) I am out of all Patience, when I look upon our Headless Paper, and see, by the Indulgence of our Patrons, LX odd,

---

30 Coffee House on St. James Street near St. James's Palace. Since Queen Anne's time, it was popular with Whig statesmen and members of Parliament. See *The Spectator*, No. 403 (June 12, 1712), for example, where Addison recounts his visits to select coffee houses to hear the speculations after a report of the death of Louis XIV, beginning with the "Fountain-head" St. James.
31 4/6 in *ECF*.
32 "transcendent": 13/39 in *ECF*.
33 "The Deformity of His Mind, as well as the Finery of His Person." *Pamela*, 6th ed. (1742), Vol. 4, p. 429.

and still scribbling [*sic*]³⁴ *on, and no manner of Likelihood that we shall ever be remember'd for a single Year to come.*

Alms-Ace, shrugging his Shoulders, answer'd, I have the Misfortune, indeed, whenever I quit my solitary Garret, and prowl among the Human Species in Search of Food, to hear every living Creature condemn our Luckless Performance, and have long despair'd of meriting the promised Rewards, and so must sink un-supported and undistinguish'd into Oblivion. But as for you Mr. Grim, and Mr. Stupid, ye have already, in Part, reap'd the Rewards of your Inborn Malice and Dulness, and the Ex----r ³⁵ *and Ex----e* ³⁶ *contribute comfortably to your Substance. And as for our younger Brother Pam', he will be happy enough, if he can but read and allow'd to boast his stupid Folly among the Templers*³⁷ *at Dick's,*³⁸ *and so be presum'd 30 Years hence capable to draw a Deed to secure to his Bookseller the Property of his future Lucubrations.* **[294]** *But I, who have tyr'd out all Mankind from my Patron Bl----t,*³⁹ *to the meanest Coffee-Man, am doom'd, I see, to be the most miserable of all* Hackney Drudges!

THE Dialogue was interrupted by the coming in of a certain *Courtier,* on whom the whole Gang voraciously fasten'd for a Dinner.

I BEG Pardon, Sir, for *hoping* you will insert this in your Paper, as well as for a farther Request I have to make to you. ---- And that is, ---- You see, Sir, the *Writers* and *their Cause* are well match'd. 'Tis impossible they should hurt you with their *impotent Malice,* and yet you may, without concerning yourself about them, do the poor Creatures great Service, and keep them from Starving, if (as sometimes you entertain the Town with the Letters of your Admirers) you will be pleased to commit those *doughty*⁴⁰ Champions to the Correction of *myself* and a *Lady of my Acquaintance.* I'll assure you, Sir, in *Pity* to them, we will spare 'em a little now and then, and not take too much Advantage of their *Ignorance* and *Blunders*: And we will endeavour at the same time to be so *concise,* as not to hinder *better Entertainment:* For a Letter once a Week or a Fortnight, Heaven knows! May easily comprehend all that is worthy even of a *Woman's Notice* in all the *Three* Papers, and be comprized in *very few* Lines too. If this

---

34 "scribbling" – 61/82 in *ECF.*
35 "Exchequer": "4.a. The office or department of the public service, which is charged with the receipt and custody of the moneys collected by the several departments of revenue." *OED.*
36 "Excise": "**1.** *gen.* Any toll or tax." *OED.*
37 "Templers": "**2.** A barrister or other person who occupies chambers in the Inner or Middle Temple." *OED.*
38 Dick's Coffeehouse near the Temple. See *The Tatler,* No. 86 (October 25–27, 1709), for detailed description.
39 Possible allusion to Edward Blount of Blagden, Devonshire (d. 1726), friend of Alexander Pope and fellow Catholic Non-juror.
40 4/9 in *ECF.*

Proposal obtain not your *Approbation,* I hope it may merit your *Excuse,* the only Motive for it being *mere Christian Charity.* For I can't be thought to propose to my self any Honour in triumphing over such weak Wretches.

I am, SIR,
Your Constant Reader and Admirer,
ATHALIAH DORMANT.

4. The True Briton. No. 45. Wednesday, November 4. 1723. [*Conscientia*]

Vol. II, pp. 390–393.

THE TRUE BRITON.
NUMB. XLV.
Parcite paucorum crimen diffundere in omnet.[41] OVID.

Monday, November 4. 1723.
The following Letter seems so pathetically, and yet with so much Temper, to bewail the unhappy *Dilemma* to which the fair Writer is reduced, on Account of the late Act of Parliament which obliges the Sex to take the Oaths, or to Register their Estates, that I cannot refuse it a Place in this Paper, though the Request contained in the last Paragraph thereof, is answered, as I conceive, by our Paper No. XLIII.
    To the TRUE BRITON.

October the 22d. 1723.

SIR,
YOU being the only Champion that appears in Publick for the Female World, and that shews any Regard to the Weak Understanding and Want of

---

41 "*Spare a few more to diffuse the crime.*"
    Prof. John F. Miller, Univ. of Virginia, who kindly helped me with this translation:

"The opening section of the third book of the *Ars amatoria*

Parcite paucarum diffundere crimen in omnes; Spectetur meritis quaeque puella suis!

'Avoid applying the crime of a few women to all of them. Let each girl be seen/ inspected for her own merits.'

Ovid goes on to say that, against the notorious Helen and Clytemnestra and others one can weigh the long faithful Penelope."

The point here is that Ovid, and indirectly the editor of this journal, advises judging women as well as men on the basis of their individual merits.

Education in our Sex, which render us uncapable of **[391]** judging of Things as, perhaps, we ought; 'tis to you we pour out our Complaints; and I, in behalf of all our afflicted Sex, beg you would represent to our Superiors, in the most moving Manner possible, the great Perplexity this late Swearing Act has put us all in. For my own Part, I am under the greatest Anxiety, having a small Fortune, and a numerous Family: If I take the Oaths required of me, I swear to Things I have no certain Knowledge of; and the Author of *The Whole Duty of Man* tells me (Page the 100) "If I swear to the Truth of that whereof I am only doubtful, though the Thing should happen to be true; yet it brings upon me the Guilt of Perjury; for I swear at a Venture, and the Thing might, for ought I know, be as well false as true; whereas I ought never to swear any thing the Truth of which I do not certainly know."[42] Then how shall I do this great Wickedness, and sin against God? I, that am wholly ignorant of what I am to swear, and have not Sense to judge of the Rights and Power of Parliament, which may make Things, to men of Sense, appear in a quite different Light? And if I neglect to take these Oaths, my little pretty Babes may want Subsistance [*sic*]; for 'tis with the utmost Care and Frugality that I at present maintain them, and cannot possibly do it if there be the least Diminution of my Fortune. What Course shall I then take? Shall I give them Bread at the Expence of my own Quiet and Conscience? or, Shall I see them want? 'Tis what no tender Mother can bear the Thought of.

AND this is not all our Grievance neither; for many of us have Husbands so zealous in this Affair, that they swear (for you know that is common with Men) **[392]** if we do not take these Oaths, they will never see our Faces more. Here is a Division made between Man and Wife, *and them whom God hath join'd, let no Man put asunder.*[43] 'Tis impossible to tell you all our Troubles: Let it suffice, that we have a Thousand Uneasinesses within, and continual Broils without; *Husbands* against *Wives, Fathers* against *Daughters*, &c.; so that I almost believe (though don't care to swear) the World to be near its End.

WHAT have we done? Or, What can we do? That we should have this Hardship laid upon our Sex? A Sex so helpless and defenceless, that, had we the Inclination (as far be it from us) 'tis not in our Power to offend. We cannot take up Arms ourselves, and we have no Influence over the Men 'tis plain, if we had, this Act had never pass'd: Or if we would give our whole Estates to assist a Rebellion, our Sex would hardly be trusted with the Secret. Does not this Act, Sir, rather give Encouragement to our Enemies Abroad, who will imagine our State in a Sinking Way, when we catch at Straws to support it;

---

42 Richard Allestree, *The Whole Duty of Man, Laid Down in a Plain and Familiar Way* (London, 1706), p. 100.
43 Mark 10:9.

(for what can the Help of a Woman's Oath be more?) No, let our Superiors despise such mean Assistance, and repeal this Act; give Ease to our tender Consciences, and thereby ingage the Hearts of all the *British* Females.[44]

BUT if there is no Pity, no Compassion due to our Weakness, Ignorance, and want of Judgment, and we (though of the establish'd Church) must have less Favour than the *Quakers*,[45] I beg Sir, you would let us know, Who by this Act are obliged to swear? Whether those only that are in Possession of their **[393]** Estates? Or, Whether Wives must swear for their Joyntures, or for any Reversionary Estates, tho' we may never live to enjoy them? For at our Tea-Tables we are much divided about it: And, dear *Britons*, assist us all you can in this Affair, and you shall for ever have the Prayers of

Your Admirer,

CONSCIENTIA.

"give ease to" 3/3 in *ECF*.
"engage the hearts" – 1 /2 in *ECF*.

5. *The True Briton.* No. 47. Monday, November 11. 1723. [*Misericordia*]

Vol. II, pp. 408–415.

To the Author of the TRUE BRITON.

SIR,

SINCE we are oblig'd to take the Oaths, I cannot help thinking that our Sex makes a much more considerable Figure in this Kingdom, than it ever did before.[46]

---

44 The term *"British* females" seems to be rare at this date and hence emphasizes all the more the radical demand of women not hitherto allowed a political voice being required to participate in these oaths. Supposedly it was always the national boast that English women were personally free of any political repression. See Henry Fielding, *Tom Jones* (1749), for instance: "In enjoying, therefore, such Place of Rendezvous, the *British* Fair ought to esteem themselves more happy than any of their foreign Sisters; as I do not remember either to have read in History, or to have seen in my Travels, any thing of the like Kind." *Tom Jones* (1749), 6 Vols., Vol. 1, Book 2, Chapter 4, p. 100.

45 Allusion to the Quaker Act pf 1721 that exempted this religious sect from taking oaths of allegiance. See above, *TB*, No. 21.

46 "The most striking aspect of the 1723 returns is the frequent presence on rolls of large numbers of women subscribers, accounting for 44 per cent of names on the return for the city of York for example. Both features of these returns—the high numbers of

I MUST farther own it frankly, to be gravely and sincerely my Opinion, That, as we are become, by such solemn Engagements, significant Members of the Body Politick, we have a kind of Right and Claim to communicate our Thoughts upon Matters relating to the Publick Welfare with as much Freedom as any *Male-Briton* whatsoever.

[409]

I DO not know what Single Men may think, but all Married Men must know, that, where our Interests are equally concerned, we Women ever thought ourselves equally privileged to declare our Sentiments, especially if we apprehended any great Grievances from our Silence.

The whole Sex must be obliged to own your Extraordinary Complaisance in this Point, since you freely indulge us with the Favour of being your Correspondents, and speaking our Minds publickly upon those Affairs which publickly concern us.

YET, though we are made happy in this Liberty, we express ourselves wholly in Complaints, without taking the more proper Method of explaining what we could reasonably propose or desire, to put an End to those Complaints. The whole Sex seems to be overwhelm'd, as it were, with a Deluge of Sorrow and Confusion; and though there are so many Thousands of them, that are as political as the Men in their own private Affairs, there has not been one, that has given herself Time to think of a proper Expedient to lay before the Great Men for their Relief in this general Perturbation and Hurry; so true is that Saying, *That what is every Body's Business, is seldom made the Business of any one Body whatsoever.*[47]

THE Case of the afflicted Lady *CONSCIENTIA*, which you lately published, was, indeed, but very lately my own unhappy Case. ---- I am a Widow, whom Fortune has bless'd with pretty comfortable Possessions; but I have several Young Children, **[410]** and, I must own, I was a long Time perplex'd with the same Doubts and Difficulties of Conforming to the Oaths, with which that unfortunate Lady (I heartily pity her!) is still making a hard Struggle.

THE Fear and Dread that a Conscience truly Scrupulous has of entring into such solemn Engagements as Oaths upon any Subject of which the Certainty is above the Reach of its Enquiries, is not to be express'd by the Pen

---

women signing and the extraordinary level of detail about subscribers on some rolls—are, it will be suggested, a product of the combined financial and political aspects of the Oaths Act," Vallance, "Women, Politics and the 1723 Oaths of Allegiance to George I," p. 981.

47 Cf. [Daniel Defoe], *Everybody's Business is Nobody's Business: Or, Private Abuses, Public Grievances Exemplified* (1725).

of the most wise and judicious Man alive, however, some Simple and Vain Men are pleas'd to ridicule it; and, therefore, how hard is it to be endured by the Heart of a poor weak and ignorant Woman? Again, the Fear and Affection which a tender Mother bears to the Offspring of her own Bowels, in their younger Years especially, are such delicate and exquisite Touches of Nature, as it is not within the Power of Man even to conceive. ---- How much greater are the Emotions and the Pangs of the Soul upon these Occasions, than the Body feels in bringing them forth with hardest Labour? Imagine then, if it be possible you should imagine, what must be the Struggle between the *Conscience* of a Mother at this Time, which on the one Hand, dreads complying with the Oaths for fear of endangering her Soul; and her Worldly Terror on the other Hand, of being deemed guilty for Non-compliance to take them; the Shocking Consequence of which represents to her, Herself and her poor Infants, through the Means of *Her* who should by Nature nourish and protect them, exposed to the Peril of a Perishing Condition ---- Dear BRITON, You *may* guess at this Extremity of Anguish ---- It is *barely* possible that you may *faintly* guess at it! ---- But I have *felt* it; and therefore **[411]** *Nature* calls upon me to plead for those, who are in your Conscientia's Case, and feel it *still*.

IT is true, as for myself, I overcame these Difficulties, and being convinced by the Reasons that follow, took the Oaths, and am now intirely at Ease with regard to my own Person; and yet not *so intirely* at Ease neither, but that I every now and then feel great Pain, when a whole Circle of beautiful Ladies, with whose Acquaintance and frequent Visits I am honour'd, and whom I know to be prudent and virtuous, and well-affected to the Government, refuse, after I have laid before them all the most cogent Reasons I can, and that induced me to take them.

ONE Day when the fair Assembly met together, I ventured to accuse Prudentia of not acting according to the Discretion she was reputed to have, for not taking the Oaths as I advised her. She answered me with much Modesty, That she did not set up for the Reputation of Wisdom, and that in the Sense we were speaking, she would rather be *Spiritually Innocent,* than *Worldly Wise;* That she was tender of doing Wrong, and scrupulous of acting what she did not understand, and binding herself under the most solemn Oaths to declare any Thing a *Certainty,* tho' she knew it to be the *greatest Probability* in the World. I then replyed, that she was not certain of her own Conscience; but that it was a Thing certain, that she must obey the Government; and therefore, according to an Archbishop's Words, *She ought to reject that doubtful Conscience, and stick to the latter, which was undoubted.* To this she reply'd, That her own Conscience must be her Judge, and either accuse **[412]** or acquit her; and consequently, that it must be her *only* Guide.⁴⁸ I then told her, That as several Learned Men had agreed on the like Occasion, she might very well suspect her own Conscience to be erroneous, because she alone, at that Rate, would seem to controll all the Wisdom of the Greatest and Learnedest Men of the whole Realm, who had made and taken it. Prudentia reply'd, That all Divines agreed to what Conscientia quotes out of the Author of the *Whole Duty of Man,* viz. *That if I swear to the Truth of that whereof I am only doubtful, though the Thing should happen to be true, yet it brings upon me the Guilty of Perjury,* &c.⁴⁹ And some Divines, said she, have not even agreed to take the Oaths; So that I, concluded she, have the Majority of Learned Men *for* me, and not *against* my Opinion.

TO this I must own, I could not make an immediate Answer: Upon which Simplicia and Innocentia, Two Beautiful and Virtuous Young Ladies, added immediately, That they were too Young to know as a *Certainty* what they apprehended they were to swear; and therefore, would not comply: But that they would willingly swear at the same Time, *That their not taking the Oaths, was not out of any Enmity to the Government*; for which they declared, and I believe they had, an Affection: But that it was *purely* because they had not a *full* and *perfect Certainty* of what they were to swear by those Oaths; and therefore were afraid of Endangering their Souls. And then very wisely censuring those, who, in an impious Sense, say, They would sooner trust *God* with their *Souls,* than *Men* with their *Estates,* they averr'd, with Tears in their **[413]** Eyes, That they were afraid they must lose their Expectations in this World.

I MUST own to you, Dear Briton, that notwithstanding I am in the main convinced that I have done right in what I have done, and can answer it to my own Conscience with Safety, (or else I would not have done it to preserve my own, or even to obtain the greatest Fortunes and Honours in the World) yet such Discourses falling from the Lips of these certainly Innocent, though mistaken People, shock me strangely at Times, and ruffle and discompose that Calm of Soul which I have always studied to preserve from all such troublesome Invasions. And indeed, when I have argued down my own Mind into Peace again, by the Means of further Reflection, I cannot still help feeling a very sensible Compassion for such tender Consciences as cannot get over

---

48 *Prudentia* is actually in agreement with Archbishop Wake's emphasis on a good conscience: "there is a *Conscience void of Offence, towards God, and towards Man;* there must be a continual plenitude of *Peace,* and *Satisfaction.* [...]The World may oppose him, but *God will be with him,*" William Wake, *Sermons Preached upon Several Occasions,* 3 Vols. (London, 1722), Vol. 3, p. 123.

49 Among the numerous editions of this household favorite, see, for instance, Allestree, *The Whole Duty of Man,* p. 100.

these Doubts. It is certain, they deserve Respect from all honest Hearts, since, if it is their Error to shrink from the Oaths which with Safety they might embrace, yet as *they* think not so, it is, methinks, not only a *pardonable,* but a beautiful Error in the *Virtuous Blind,* that they are so *tenderly* afraid of wounding their Consciences with the least Remorse.

OUT of Persons, who have such honestly formed and such piously regulated Minds, and who scruple to do the least Thing which may offend that *Inward Judge* of both our Honour and Virtue called *Conscience*; Out of them, I say, are to be chosen the *best Friends,* The most *sincere Companions,* The *kindest Mistresses* of *Families,* The most *faithful Servants,* The *tenderest Mothers,* The most *obedient Daughters,* **[414]** The *best-natur'd Sisters,* and The most *endearing Wives:* In fine, The most *ornamental* and *beneficial* Members of every Class of Society upon Earth. Must it not then be painful to a generous Mind to consider, that such People particularly, above all the rest of the World, should be made liable to any Distress upon Account of that *very Tenderness* of *Conscience*; however mistaken in *one Thing,* that makes them so eminently valuable in *all* the other Stations, and in *every other* Duty of Life.

THIS, if Female Politcks might avail, has put me upon racking my Thoughts to find, Whether I could form an acceptable Scheme for their Relief; and I think I have at last found out one very practicable Method, by which the Women may be obliged to take an Oath, which would at one and the same Time, be equally consistent with the Security of the Government, as if they took all the Oaths now prescribed, and yet not all obnoxious to the Tenderest of their own Consciences.

WHAT I would humbly propose, is, That those who are too scrupulous to take the Oaths in the Form they are now administered, may swear, That they do not refuse them out of Obstinacy; That they do not refuse them because they either are, or will be involved in the Guilt of bearing any *Civil Enmity* against the Government; but purely for the Sake of *Conscience,* as being loth to swear what they do not *Positively* and *Absolutely* know for a *Certainty.*

THIS would as effectually bind them to be good Subjects, as all the Oaths now offer'd to them; and all that take this Oath may be depended upon to swear Truth; or, if not, how could they be more depended **[415]** upon by taking any others, though even a Thousand in Number?

HOW many Uneasy Families would this quiet? How many disturb'd Consciences would it calm? To how many restless and innocent Ladies would this Procedure of our Men in Authority and Power, give Content?

THE Lords and Commons of *England* are such Fine Gentlemen, that they have always passed for the Ladies of this Kingdom, Laws which are more favourable to the Sex than are to be found establish'd by any other Assembly of Legislators under the Heavens.

THE Reverend Bench of Bishops would infallibly come into any reasonable Method, as this certainly is, of giving Consciences truly scrupulous all possible Satisfaction: So that, methinks, this Project needs nothing but being known, to be put in Execution to the Content of every TRUE BRITON; and therefore I chuse to communicate it by the Means of your Paper; In which if you give it a Place you will oblige,

Your Admirer,

MISERICORDIA.

"proper expedient" 1/1 in *ECF.*

"to speak her mind" 3 /4

"cogent reason" 1 /2

"tender consciences" 3 /4

"scruple to do" 4/5

6. *The True Briton.* No. 61. Monday, December 30. 1723. [*Old Batchelor*]

Vol. II, pp. 523–524.

To the TRUE BRITON.

SIR,

I AM one, who have hitherto, entertain'd such a frightful Notion of *Matrimony*, that nothing has been able to draw me into it. So many discouraging *Proverbs* as we have relating to that State, and so many more discouraging *Examples*, in which I have seen them verify'd, have made me often resolve within **[524]** myself to live and die as I am. But since the late Act of Parliament obliging the Female Sex to take the Oaths to the Government, I begin to think, I might, by the Assistance of the Legislature, mend my own Condition, and many of Theirs into the Bargain.

FOR this Purpose, I intend, at the ensuing Sessions, to endeavour to get a Bill brought in, requiring all Women, before they are Married, and as a Part of the Ceremony, to take an Oath of *Allegiance*, and another allowing the *Supremacy* to their Husbands. This seems to me very likely to pass both Houses of Parliament; and especially, because there are some Instances, wherein, by the Laws of *England*, Women are already adjug'd guilty of Treason for Facts committed against their *Husbands*.[50] And I am willing to leave it intirely to that Wise Body of Men, Whether the Bill shall have *Retrospect*,[51] so as to oblige all Women *already Married,* to take the same Oaths.

WHAT your Condition may be, I know not; But I am apt to think, that the Design, when *You* make it publick, will be well taken by *many* a *True Briton.*
I am, SIR,
Your Friend and Admirer,
OLD BATCHELOR.[52]

7. *The True Briton.* No. 71. Monday, February 3. 1723-4. [*Violette*]

Vol. II, pp. 607–609.

To the TRUE BRITON.

SIR,

'TIS with Pleasure I find many of our Reverend Clergy, and the *whole Bench* of Bishops join to decry the *Masquerades,* and interpose their Authority to prevent the Ladies of *Great Britain,* being expos'd to the Attacks of their Footmen. I am not so ill-natur'd and uncharitable as to believe that all the Women who go to a *Masquerade,* are dishonest. Every one may see it once, as they would a *Monster*; but after their Curiosity is gratify'd, there must be other Pleasures in View to make it deserve the Name even of a *Diversion.* The Unseasonable **[608]** Hours; The promiscuous Company; The Unbounded Freedoms of the Place; The inspiring Liquors, and tempting Viands, and the unbridled Liberties of Converse, are strange Temptations, and fit for very few who are

---

50 "**petty treason** *n.* now *historical* the crime of murdering someone to whom the murderer owed allegiance, such as a master or husband." *OED.* " 'Tis true, should a Wife be so audacious as to find Means to confine her Husband, she would be unpardonable; her Guilt would be aggravated by the Relation she stands in to him, by the Respect and Deference she owes him; it would be a kind of *Petty Treason*," [Sarah Chapone], *The Hardships of the English Laws in Relation to Wives,* ed. Susan Paterson Glover (London and New York: Routledge, 2018), p. 32.

51 "1728 E. CHAMBERS *Cycl.* at *Retroactive* We have some Instances of Laws that have a Retrospect, or Retroaction, i.e. were made with express Design to extend to things already pass'd." *OED.*

52 See the more extensive portrait of this iconic satirical character in *The Weekly Miscellany.* No. 304. (October 21, 1738). William Congreve (1670-1729)'s first play, *The Old Batchelor,* first performed in London's Drury Lane in 1693, with music by Henry Purcell, was an enormous success. *ODNB.*

not abandon'd to the Luxuries of a most degenerate Age,[53] and cannot act a Part in the blackest and most criminal Parts of corrupted Life.

THE Ladies should consider, that 'tis nothing but *strict Virtue*, and a *decent Reservedness*, that keeps their Sex from falling into Contempt; and they ought not to lay aside an Appearance that gains them Respect, and keeps in Awe Mankind, who are ever designing on their Virtue, to take up one, that exposes them to the rough Address of every sordid Fellow.

THE Freedoms of a *Masquerade* are but very indifferent Methods of initiating fine young Ladies into Conversation, when they have taken Leave of their Governesses, and find themselves freed from those strict Rules of Virtue and Morality, which are too apt to sit uneasy on the Gay and the Youthful Part of the Sex, which therefore is more susceptible of Impressions of a contrary Nature. Thus prepar'd, and falling into the Ribaldries of a *Masquerade*, what Improvement may not be expected from the Minds of ductile Youth? *Excessive Liberties* naturally bring on *Excessive Restraints*:[54] and 'twill be found proper in Time, perhaps, to immure the Sex as in *Turkey*, and other Parts, to confine those Bodies, whose Minds are too apt to be gadding after such enormous Diversions.

[609]

THE Sex had so many Varieties and Foibles before, that *Celibacy* was never so common, nor *Matrimony* more despis'd; and in a while, the sober Part of Mankind will unanimously disclaim the Tie that gives them a Chance so unequal to their Merits, and exposes their Beds to the Intrigues and Pollutions of abandon'd Rakes and Jilting Coquettes; and then the Sex may thank themselves for becoming a Prey,[55] both Persons and Fortunes, for want

---

53 "The Fashion from large Hoops so enormous that the Head of a Family will find he must buy the same Quantity of Rich Silks for his Daughters as would have served, before that indecent and unnatural Fashion came up, and which, in the present Age of Luxury, seems to be continued rather, for the Sake of the Expence, than for general Approbation's Sake," SR to Frances Grainger (September 8, 1750), *The Correspondence with Sarah Wescomb, Frances Grainger, and Laetitia Pilkington* (2015), ed. John A. Dussinger (*Cambridge Edition of the Correspondence of Samuel Richardson*) (Cambridge: Cambridge University Press), pp. 338–339.

54 "Then, as to the great article of fidelity to your bed, are not women of family, who are well-educated, under greater restraints, than creatures, who, if they ever had reputation, sacrifice it to sordid interest, or to more sordid appetite, the moment they give up to you? Does not the example you furnish, of having succeeded with her, give encouragement for others to attempt her likewise? For, with all her blandishments, can any man be so credulous." *Clarissa*, 3rd ed. (1751), Vol. 4, p 88.

55 "Yet *my teazing ways*, it seems, *are intolerable*. --- Are women only to teaze, I trow? ---The Sex may thank themselves for teaching me to out-teaze them." *Clarissa*, 3rd ed. (1751), Vol. 4, pp. 181–182.

of better Offers, to the harden'd Attempts of *Irish* Impudence, whose natural Talent is *Masquerading* in every Part of Life. You will excuse me this Warmth of Expression, which is owing to the utter Ruin of a dear Kinswoman, whose ample Fortunes and blooming Beauties are destroy'd and blasted by successful Villainy and corroding Diseases, the Consequences of an Intrigue that began *last Masquerading Time*. If you please to insert this Letter, you will oblige many of your Female Country Readers, and in particular,

Your Humble Servant,

VIOLETTE.

"designing on" 1/1 in *ECF.*

"exposes them" 2/3

"fine young ladies" 2/2

"naturally bring" 1 /2

"too apt to be" 6/8

"the Sex may thank themselves" 1/1

"natural Talent" 2 /4

"ample Fortunes" 2/2

"better offers" 1/1

Chapter 3

INTRODUCTION TO *THE WEEKLY MISCELLANY*: SARAH CHAPONE, WOMEN'S "CHAMPIONESS"

1. William Webster and Richardson

If, as printer of the *True Briton,* Richardson took considerable risks to support the Duke of Wharton's campaign against Walpole's government, his work for the improvident clergyman William Webster (1689–1758) reveals again how seriously he regarded the press as a medium equivalent to the pulpit in promulgating the business of the state church.

> *The Weekly Miscellany,* edited by William Webster, under the pseudonym of *Richard Hooker of the Temple,* was published Saturdays from 16 December 1732 through 27 June 1741 as a single sheet. Richardson printed the first 209 issues, the last on 11 December 1736. [...] A letter from Webster admits that at the time of writing (15 July 1738) he still owed Richardson the sum of ninety pounds, a debt Richardson generously later forgave.[1]

As we shall see while tracing his own interventions in this journal, besides his genuine concern for poor clergymen, it is not unlikely that Richardson valued the ample opportunity this journal provided him as a developing writer and a means of advertising his publications.

Webster himself confessed that he was seduced by Richardson's fictional female voice: "while you are alive you can, whenever you please, make any body Cry, or Laugh; and when you Die, you'll make Every body Cry whether you write, or not."[2] A few years after this remark, while undergoing bankruptcy and failing to get relief from the archbishops and bishops, Webster wrote A *Plain Narrative of Facts, or, the Author's Case Fairly and Candidly Stated, By*

---

1 Maslen, p. 30.
2 William Webster to SR, November 26, 1753, after reading *Sir Charles Grandison,* FM XV, 3, f, 18.

Way of Appeal to the Publick. After profuse thanks to a parishioner for his financial support, Webster singles out

> another Person, not the less honourable for not being a *Gentleman,* who is absolutely the greatest Genius, the best and the most amiable Man, that I know in the World; I mean, Mr. *Richardson,* the Printer. When I came to *Ware,* I was £90 in his Debt, tho' I had clear'd off regularly, by quarterly Payments, £50, and never could save any Thing out of my Income ever since the Change of my Livings, towards getting out of Debt. As soon as I was possess'd of *Ware,* or, rather, as soon as *Ware* was possess'd of *me,* he sent me a kind Letter, told me, that any Sum of Money that I wanted was at my Service; and when he saw that I liv'd as *frugally* as possible, he forgave me the whole Debt. I forbear to inlarge upon his Character, because I know not how to do it Justice.[3]

Worth emphasis is the point that Webster's thrift was a condition of Richardson's benevolence. At issue at this time was the scandalous inequality in sharing the state church revenue, where landowners held the power over benefices and could award multiple livings to their preferred clergyman. Richardson was deeply concerned about the plight of the many Anglican curates without income unless lucky enough to find a rich patron or wife. His friendship with Richard Newton, the principal of Hart Hall in Oxford, who strove to reform the curriculum and reduce the annual expenses of an undergraduate, was similar in motive. While printing Newton's *Pluralities indefensible. A treatise humbly offered to the consideration of the parliament of Great Britain. By a Presbyter of the Church of England* (1743), Richardson enlists the newly married *Pamela* as an advocate for *Mr. Williams,* invoking the argument in this tract:

> Tell us, *Pamela,* said Mr. B., whether you do not intend this as a Satire upon the Practice, or is it really your pretty Ignorance, that has made you pronounce one of the severest Censures upon it, that could be thought of?
>
> I smiled; and said, Indeed, Sir, I think only some such Reason, or a worse, must be the Original of Dispensations: For is it right, that One Gentleman shall have Two or Three Livings, the Duties of no more than One of which he can personally attend, while so many are destitute of Bread, almost, and exposed to Contempt, the too frequent Companions of Poverty?[4]

---

3 *A Plain Narrative of Facts, or, the Author's Case Fairly and Candidly Stated, By Way of Appeal to the Publick* (London, 1750), p. ii.
4 Maslen, pp. 537–538. *Pamela,* Vol. 3, p. 345.

Webster's basic aim in editing the *Weekly Miscellany* was to advance the views of the High Church and Non-juror against the perceived decline in religion. It was not by chance that Richardson was asked to be its printer in 1732, whose shop had already produced an array of such jeremiads as *The Apprentice's Vade Mecum, The Infidel Convicted,* and *Two Letters from a Deist to His Friend* (1730).[5] But as usual, when undertaking a contract, Richardson immediately engaged in strategies to enhance the product's public reception, and a journal devoted to reviewing the many religious tracts of the day seemed unlikely to attract many in the laity. It is probable, therefore, that he had a share in choosing the pen name *Richard Hooker* to give some comic distance to the editorial narrative. From the outset of this printing project, Richardson seems to have dreaded the opprobrium of enthusiasm that earned a place in Pope's *Dunciad*, II, l. 258. Despite Webster's religious sincerity, Richardson distrusted him as an ambassador of the church. When trying to increase his acquaintance with Mark Hildesley, for instance, he regretted having asked Webster to apologize for his silence: "My friend [Webster], I am afraid, was too grave in delivering my Hint."[6] From his autobiographical remark, Richardson probably feared the same tendency in his own behavior: "I was not fond of Play, as other Boys; My Schoolfellows used to call me *Serious* and *Gravity*."[7]

Already when editing *The Oxford Methodists*, a basic tenet in Richardson's faith opposes the idea that "Religion was design'd to contradict Nature";[8] he emphasizes instead that it is the only way to fulfill our imperfect nature. *Pamela*'s condemnation of puritanical behavior is on the same grounds: "I said, that this Over-gloominess was not Religion, I was persuaded; but either Constitution or Mistake; and I was sorry always when I met with it; for tho'

---

5 Dussinger, "Fabrications from Samuel Richardson's Press." *Papers for the Bibliographical Society*, Vol. 100, No. 2 (2006), pp. 259–279.
6 *Correspondence with Lady Bradshaigh and Lady Echlin*, 3 Vols. (Cambridge Edition of the Correspondence of Samuel Richardson), ed. Peter Sabor (Cambridge: Cambridge University Press, 2016), SR to Lady Echlin (July 24, 1754), Vol. 2, p. 474.
7 John Carroll, ed., *Selected Letters of Samuel Richardson* (Oxford: Clarendon, 1964), p. 231 and p. 340.
8 "They [Oxford Methodists] continued their Services to the poor Prisoners; visited such of their Acquaintance as were sick, and several poor Families besides in Town, and made Collections from the Well-disposed, and among one another, to procure Physick, and other Reliefs to the bodily Necessities, as by their best Advice and Prayers they did to the Spiritual Wants, where needed; and abridg'd themselves of some Diversions and Pleasures, in order to enable them to support the Expence which attended this good Course; and not, as the Gentleman assur'd me, from any melancholy Habit, or Gloominess of Disposition, which this Method had brought them, into: For, as he declar'd, Religion is a cheerful Thing, and the Satisfactions they reaped from the Sense of having perform'd what they took to be their Duty, however imperfectly, were greater, and of a higher Nature, than any they had ever before experienc'd," pp. 7–8.

it might betoken a pious Mind, it certainly shew'd a narrow one, and I fear'd did more Harm than Good."[9] Even Lovelace himself knows that a spiritual conversion does not necessarily mean becoming a Puritan: "Dost thou not know, that Religion, if it has taken proper hold of the heart, is the most chearful countenance-maker in the world?"[10]

2. *Belinda* as *Hooker*'s Helpmeet

Webster's description of the playful fictional voices that intersperse the extensive theological discourse of this journal seems to echo Richardson himself: "Our Correspondence is something like a Conversation in Masquerade, but enter'd into with more innocent Intentions, and carried on with more Modesty than those Nocturnal Dialogues are," *WM*, No. 243 (August 19, 1737). In view of Richardson's female impersonations while editing *The True Briton*, Belinda entered the *Weekly Miscellany* as another means of attracting female readers to the journal. This pseudonym obviously alludes to the heroine of Pope's mock-epic *The Rape of the Lock*. Richardson had already printed John Dennis's *Remarks on Mr. Pope's RAPE OF THE LOCK* (1728).[11] No matter how popular Pope's poem may have been, it helps to know that Richardson himself printed this pamphlet dealing critically with this work and its focus on *Belinda* as a stereotype of a fashionable woman. Richardson's "feminist" Belinda is introduced as an ironic contrast to Pope's misogynistic stereotype.

Unlike the clueless mannequin of the aristocratic world, this *Belinda* is well-informed and does not hesitate to give advice about the marketability of *Hooker*'s journal: "I must therefore take the honest Freedom to tell you, if you write to the Publick, you must a little consult the Taste of the Publick, or your Lectures will stand a bad Chance, either to lie peaceably at the Publisher's, or to rest as peaceably upon the Table." Again, we have a printer's concern with adequate circulation, just as *Athalia Dormant* expressed in the *True Briton*, No. 34 (September 27, 1723). In a postscript to *Belinda*'s first appearance in the *Weekly Miscellany*, Hooker praises her wit as being compatible with the serious discourse elsewhere in the journal:

> I am obliged to Belinda for reminding me, that Good nature and Benevolence in a Writer will be of the greatest Force to recommend

---

9 *Pamela*, 6th ed. (1742), Vol. 3, p. 264.
10 *Clarissa*, 3rd ed. (1751), Vol. 8, p. 188.
11 Maslen, p. 239. See *WM*, No. 299 (September 15, 1738), for *Belinda*'s explicit contrast to Pope's stereotype of the fashionable coquette.

his Writings, be they of what Kind they will, and that the finest Compositions will be disgustful and ineffectual, as to any good Influence on the Reader, when an Author writes, not that he may do good to others by his Instructions, but to ease himself by discharging a proper Quantity of Gall and Ire. *WM*, No. 27 (June 16, 1733)

Perhaps the most original and insightful character trait is not only her business sense in promoting the journal's readership but also her continual awareness of keeping a high enough standard of writing as a woman newcomer. At the end of her career, in the *WM*, No. 421 (January 17, 1740), when Fielding was launching *The Champion* and introduced *Captain Hercules Vinegar*, *Belinda* rejected this satiric character's attempts to defend women's rights while assuming her name:

In short, he has lately put on *Pinners* and a *Petticoat*; and any one might easily guess what a staring, frightful Figure, the *Champion* of *England*, the *Hercules* of the Age, must make in *female Attire*, and what a Disgrace he has done us by such a monstrous Representation. But not content with doing Dishonour to our Persons, he has brought Infamy upon our Characters, by talking as filthily as he looks. A Bawd in Breeches, canting about Regeneration and the Pangs of the New Birth, or a Debauchee in a Gown and Cassock, preaching up Repentance and a pious Life, could not act a more unnatural Part, or act it more awkwardly. As a *Woman* I resent it, in Honour of my Sex. But he has offended and injured me in a particular Manner, by assuming my *Name* too; the more because, as I have taken in his Paper, his nasty Performance will be the more likely to pass for mine, by those who are not acquainted with me, and give the envious Prude an Occasion for Scandal, and the wanton Flirt an Example to justify her immodest Freedoms. Besides, tho' I was not in a Humour to continue a Correspondence with you, I would not have 'Squire *Hooker* think *Belinda* would discard him for any other Champion. You are engaged in a nobler Cause, and better deserve **[middle column]** the Title than any of your Brethren, as well a better answer it. As it is the Business of [a] *Champion* to engage the *Enemies* of his Country, and of an *Hercules* to rid the World of *Monsters*, you attack our *greatest* Enemies and the *greatest* Monsters that can infest and ravage a Nation, the Enemies of *Religion* and *Virtue*;[12] But *Captain Vinegar* attacks

---

12 Alludes to *The Champion* (January 1, 1739–40).

the Honour of the *Fair*, whom all true Warriors have thought themselves obliged to defend, and makes himself a Greater Monster than the GREAT *Hercules* himself ever subdued. Be pleased, therefore, to let the *Captain* know that it was below his Character to put a Parcel of little smutty Stuff into the Mouth of a Lady, and a Piece of Injustice to affix to it the Name of your much injur'd

BELINDA.

As if fearful that Webster's readers might actually fall for Fielding's ruse, she adds a further defense:

P. S. Let anyone look into my Letters published in the two Volumes of the *Miscellanies*, and see whether I have been used to write in such an impudent Manner.

Thanks to *Belinda*, the path is now cleared for the historical contretemps between the authors of *Pamela* and of *Shamela*, respectively.

In her first letter to the *WM*, No. 27 (June 16, 1733), *Belinda* renders a detailed Hogarthian scene of how the journal is received in her home, which she shares with a puritanical guardian who thrives on religious gloom:

I live with an old Maiden Aunt, who mightily likes the Piety of your Design, and the Gravity of your Performances. She longs for the coming in of the Post with as much Impatience as I should expect a Letter from my Lover. As soon as the Letter-Carrier knocks at the Door (which is generally in the Evening) the Candles, the Curate, and Miss are call'd for in great haste. When the good old Gentlewoman has properly placed a little Instrument to her Ear, and the Reverend Gentleman has fixed another upon his Nose, your dry Discourse is bawled out with a Voice as loud as would reach the largest Church in your City, and in a Tone as canting as any that was in Fashion in the Times of old Noll.[13] If any Part be duller; I ask your Pardon, good Sir, I mean graver, than ordinary, it is sure to strike their Want of Fancy, and we must needs have it over again. I shall dread the Sound of Encore as much as a dying Wretch trembles at the Toll of his passing Bell.

Webster's "Gravity" may be gratifying to a sickly old maid, but *Belinda* implies how a young and healthy audience might react. Twenty years later, Richardson is still deploring his "grave" friend's way of discussing religion. As

---

[13] Nickname for Oliver Cromwell (1599–1658), Lord Protector of the Commonwealth of England, Scotland, and Ireland (1653–58).

if this satiric piece missed the point, *Belinda*'s second and third letters repeat the warning about *Hooker*'s lack of humor, *WM*, No. 42 (September 29, 1733) and No. 53 (December 15, 1733).

Besides this overall concern with the journal's reception, throughout the eight subsequent letters, *Belinda* focuses on four issues: (1) the contempt of the clergy and its root in the inequality of livings (*WM*, Nos. 180, 186, 252); (2) courtship and marriage (*WM*, Nos. 180, 186, 198, 272); (3) women's rights, women writers, Sarah Chapone (*WM*, Nos. 198, 272, 353, 421); and (4) defense of religious orthodoxy and attack on infidelity and enthusiasm (*WM*, Nos. 180, 364, 421). While invoking such topics of the current discourse, Richardson fleshes out the character of *Belinda* as a humorous observer of events who continually takes part in the passing scene and anticipates the ironic roles played by the leathery *Anna Howe* and *Charlotte Grandison* in their disputations.[14]

---

14 *WM*, No. 180 (May 29, 1736). [*Belinda*'s 4th letter]—marriage proposal to Hooker as means of getting him into orders and being able to afford being a clergyman.

WM, No. 186 (July 17, 1736). [*Belinda*'s 5th letter] – ironic response to Hooker's silence about proposal, implies he is typical *Old Batchelor*.

WM, No. 198 (October 9, 1736). [*Belinda*'s 6th letter] – *Belinda*'s aunt's dream about her possible married states. Scenario of young marriageable woman with an elderly aunt whose moral approval is required for her giving consent to a suitor: *Familiar Letters* (1750), *LETTER LXXI*, pp. 100–101. [Same situation with the suitor trying to impress the aunt so that he can successfully court her niece.] *LETTER LXXXIV*, aunt advising niece to accept a morally impeccable suitor with the hopes of her improving her own behavior by such a marriage, pp. 117–119. *Clarissa Harlowe* reflects on her plight in a family where even her aunt has not been able to exert her authority in preventing her being forced into a bad marriage, *Clarissa*, 3rd ed. (1751), Vol. 7, p. 226. *Aunt Selby* as paragon of family matron, *Grandison*, 3rd ed. (1754), Vol. 1, pp. 27–28. *Harriet* recommends *Emily Jervois* to depend on Aunt Selby for an exemplary mentor, *Grandison* (1754), Vol. 7, p. 271.

WM, No. 252 (October 21, 1737). [*Belinda*'s 7th letter] – *Belinda* promises to make *Hooker* her heir as a means of supporting him as clergyman– another satiric attack on the contempt of the clergy and promise to give financial support.

WM, No. 272 (March 10, 1737–1738). [*Belinda*'s 8th letter] – Richardson's formula for securing not only young women but also young men from the deceptions inevitable in courtship to avoid the shock of recognition after marriage – on young men who deceive themselves in courtship Astell and Chapone influence?

<< *WM*, No. 243 (August 19, 1737) – Hooker's invitation to Chapone>>

WM, No. 353 (September 29, 1739). [*Belinda*'s 9th letter] – *Belinda*'s account of her own itch for writing but confesses that she is outdone by a rival writer—Sarah Chapone.

Belinda's eighth letter on self-deception in courtship and subsequent disappointment in marriage seems to draw upon Mary Astell, whose *Some Reflections upon Marriage* Richardson edited in 1730.[15] A more recent stimulus was doubtless the appearance of Sarah (*née* Kirkham) Chapone's *The Hardships of the English Laws in Relation to Wives*, published anonymously in 1735. Although one letter in the *Weekly Miscellany*, No. 132 (June 28, 1735), signed *Aspasia*, praised this vigorous feminist tract, two other reviews denounced its irreverent view of marriage, *Weekly Miscellany*, No. 300 (October 23, 1736) and No. 303 (November 13, 1736). *Aspasia* was Mary Granville's pen name in her correspondence with the Gloucestershire circle.[16] Her neighbor friend, in turn, was dubbed *Sappho*.

> About this time I contracted a friendship with Sappho, [Sarah Kirkham] a clergyman's daughter in the neighbourhood, a girl of my own age. She had an uncommon genius and intrepid spirit, which though really innocent, alarmed my father, and made him uneasy at my great attachment to her. He loved gentleness and reserve in the behaviour of women, and could not bear anything that had the appearance of being too free and masculine; but as I was convinced of her innocence, I saw no fault in Miss Kirkham. She entertained me with her wit, and she battered me with her approbation, but by the improvements she has since made, I see she was not, at my first acquaintance, the perfect creature I thought her then. We wrote to one another every day, and met in the fields between our fathers' houses as often as we had an opportunity, thought that day tedious that we did not meet, and had many stolen interviews. Her extraordinary understanding, lively imagination and humane disposition, which soon became conspicuous, at last reconciled my father to her, and he never after debarred me the pleasure of seeing her, when

---

WM, No. 364 (December 15, 1739). [*Belinda*'s 10th letter] – satiric account of two libertines who converted to Methodism [*Mr. B* converted by *Pamela* – see also *Familiar Letters* (1750), No. 76: "that still greater Libertine, Peter Mottram, Methodist."].

WM, No. 353 (September 29, 1739). [*Belinda*'s 11th letter—on death of *Delia*].

WM, No. 421 (January 17, 1740). [*Belinda*'s 12th letter] – praising Hooker for his battle against infidelity and rejecting *Captain Hercules*'s wrong-headed attempts to defend women's rights.

15 Dussinger, "Mary Astell's Revisions of *Some Reflections upon Marriage* (1730)," *Papers for the Bibliographical Society of America*, Vol. 107, No. 1 (2013), pp. 49–79.

16 See C. E. Vulliamy, *Aspasia: The Life and Letters of Mary Granville, Mrs. Delany (1700-1788)* (London: Geoffrey Bles, 1935).

it was convenient we should meet. My sister was at this time a plaything to us, and often offended at our whispers and mysterious talk.[17]

Mary Granville was a witness to the Ms. of this pamphlet that Sarah had given to John Wesley to read and may have been helpful in getting it published with a bookseller. Her share in Sarah Kirkham's close relations with Wesley at this time may have been the way Richardson managed to obtain the Wesley manuscript letter that was printed without his permission as *The Oxford Methodists* (1733, 1738). Although there is no record of Richardson's correspondence with Chapone before the 1750s, Sarah hints that they had exchanged letters since at least 1740: "my Heart has talked of you and wrote to you for above these twelve Years."[18] The fact that Richardson nowhere mentions *The Hardships* when writing to her may only confirm his reliability in keeping her authorship secret, as she had intended. Perhaps one early link was Patrick Delany. Sarah was excited about Delany's *Revelation Examined with Candour* (1732) and praised it in *Hardships*. This book was printed by Richardson, who might have sent her a copy to Gloucestershire.[19] How else did she have a copy to read? She did not have the money to buy books, and from her own words, it does not seem that Mary Granville initiated her reading this work. Ironic since she later married Delany! Sarah also references the preface to this book published separately and again printed by Richardson: *The Present State of Learning, Religion, and Infidelity in Great-Britain. Wherein the causes of the present degeneracy of taste, and increase of infidelity, are inquir'd into, and accounted for* (1732).[20]

At the conclusion of her letter, *Aspasia* offers to supply Hooker with writers who would enliven his journal:

> I have the Happiness of knowing several Ladies, who, I'm sure, can exert the same Talents, and give you very great Assistance, if you can engage them in a Correspondence. They will probably not interfere in your Disputes with the *Dissenters*, where Depth of Reading, and great Knowledge of Antiquity, are required; but as to the *Infidel* Tribe, they quitted their Reason when they quitted their Religion, and may possibly be bantered, but cannot be argued, into Sense and Good-manners.

---

17 Mrs. Delany (1700–1788), *The Autobiography and Correspondence of Mary Granville, Mrs Delany*, ed. Lady Llanover, 1st ser., 3 vols. (1861), Vol. I, pp. 15–16.
18 *FM XII, 2, ff, 46–47.* [No date, but answers SR's March 2, 1752 and answered (after a delay) April 18]
19 Maslen, pp. 228–235.
20 Maslen, p. 229. The preface to Vol. 2, but Maslen does not list the separate edition.

Granville's witty letter probably was enough to get *Hooker* to invite Sarah Chapone to contribute to the *Weekly Miscellany*. This letter *WM*, No. 243 (August 19, 1737), might have been written by Richardson himself:

> In an Age when so little Pains is taken to improve the Understandings of the Women, and so much Pains is taken to corrupt the Morals and Principles of the Men, a Lady that is capable of writing with great Strength and Perspicuity, and a Gentleman that believes his Religion, and has Zeal enough to defend it, are very great Curiosities in their kind. But as you, Madam, have shewn what the *Fair Sex* can do, whenever they think fit to exercise the fine Talents which Nature has given them, I hope Example will have some Effect towards making the 'Squires less ashamed of appearing in Defence of their Faith.

If we take Webster at his word here, he did not read *Hardships* before the two letters appeared in his *Miscellany* (October 23, 1736, and November 13, 1736). But his admiration of the pamphlet and his desire to have Chapone write more things for the *Miscellany* are unequivocal. That Richardson, as printer, did not know Chapone to be the author of *Hardships* seems very doubtful. On the contrary, his editing/printing of Astell's *Serious Reflections*, Delany's *Revelation Examined*, and Wesley's *The Oxford Methodists* in the early 1730s seems pertinent to writing her own polemic on marriage. In the introductory paragraphs to his invitation, Webster mentions how he came to know of her authorship:

> *Curiosity* lead [*sic*] me to read, and a great deal of strong Sense and Wit obliged me to admire, a Pamphlet, lately published by Mr *Roberts*, under the Title of, *The Hardships of the English Laws in Relation to Wives*. Expressing my high Opinion of the Performance and the Abilities of it's Author, it provoked a particular Friend of her's, and mine to tell me that it was a *Lady*, and that he had the Happiness of being intimately acquainted with her.

Without evidence to the contrary, it is fair to speculate that this mutual friend was Richardson.

Since Chapone was adamant about keeping anonymous, it probably gave her little comfort to find Webster publishing her reply without her permission. Again, perhaps he was not acting alone. As a printer, Richardson took such liberties when using Wesley's manuscript for *The Oxford Methodists* or Elizabeth Carter's "Ode to Wisdom" for *Clarissa*. In her ironic reply, Chapone brushes aside Webster's fulsome praise and explains that her time spent raising and teaching her children prevented her from replying to the sexist letters in the *Weekly Miscellany*. But at the end of her letter declining his invitation, Chapone hints that when the time is convenient, she may contribute something.

> After this plain artless Relation of my Circumstances, I hope Sir, that you will acquit me of the Charge of want of *Faith*, or Zeal for my Religion and Country, if I should continue to circumscribe my Inclinations, by not suffering them to carry me beyond Domestic Duties, till my Children shall no longer want my constant Care and Instruction. Whenever I can command a little Time, it shall be laid out as you require.

Six months after her reply, in the *WM*, No. 265 (January 1737/1738), a brief letter from *Somebody* praises *Hooker*'s piety and apologizes for her poor writing, and then five months later, a long and elaborate letter with this cipher gives a panoramic account of the social classes, *WM*, No. 284 (June 2, 1738). It is tempting to read these missives as a prelude to the first letter signed *Delia*, on the inequalities of marriage and the educated wife's plight while trying to raise a family with a husband lacking any respect for women, *WM*, No. 290 (July 14, 1738):

> But the Squire at length coming to Years of maturity, instead of Discretion, has already been married long enough, to be tired of his Wife; he now thinks his Running Mare a much handsomer Creature,[21] and prefers the yelping of a Hound before her talk; especially if she is so unlucky as to speak Sense. In this unhappy Situation what can be done? To reconcile them to one another is as impossible as to reconcile Light and Darkness, Wit and Folly, Sense and no Sense; But since this can't be, let them try to reconcile themselves to themselves and to their own Condition. When the Gentleman mounts his Horse for the Field, let the Lady, repair (after having given the necessary Directions to her Servants about her Family Affairs) to her new Study, and read Lessons of Patience and Obedience.[22]

---

21 "But suppose a Woman does not look upon Marriage as a common Bargain, and does not chuse to be barter'd for like a Horse or a Cow, she may chance to consider it as a religious Institution, and not as a civil Ordinance," [March 1752] Mrs. Chapone N. d., but answers *FM XII, 2, ff.* to SR his March 2, 1752 and pp. 46–57 answered (after a delay) April 18.

22 "Women were designed for *Domestick Animals*, 'tis but allotting them their proper Place; give them *Needles* and *Prayer Books* there, and there's no great harm done." *Hardships*, p. 32.

The case study approach here resembles the evidential method in *Hardships* to demonstrate failed marriages.

But why the pen name *Delia*? Although in their youthful correspondence Mary Granville (*Aspasia*) playfully addressed Sarah Kirkham as *Sappho*, the humble Gloucestershire wife, mother, and teacher would not be so pretentious as to claim the stature of the ancient Greek lyric poetess. It might be a sheer coincidence, of course, that John Duncombe's *The Feminiad* (1754) invokes this pastoral name for Sarah's daughter-in-law, Hester (née Mulso) Chapone. But then again, in that intimate circle of family members often sharing Richardson's hospitality, it may be a coded way of linking Sarah and Hester as similar feminist voices. Duncombe married Susanna Highmore in 1761 and was a prolific writer in his later years.[23] Only two months later, an unsigned letter in *WM*, No. 299 (September 1738), praises *Delia* and urges her to contribute further letters. If it had come from Webster, we could expect to see *Hooker* as the author. A stylistic comparison with Richardson's record in the Chadwyck-Healey database reveals enough similarities to risk attributing this letter to his name.

Not all of Chapone's letters to the *WM* employ this pen name.

Besides two from *Somebody*, a long letter signed *Agricola* in *WM*, No. 302 (October 6, 1738) renders a patriarchal dystopia in ancient Athens where wives owe unquestioning obedience to their husbands:

> A Woman of Condition, scarce Fifteen, and a Bride, patiently sits by the Hour together to be school'd and tutor'd in the Duty of her Station by one, who pass'd for the best natured, most virtuous and prudent Man in *Athens*, the politest City of the World; near which he lived enjoying and improving his Family Estate: But then, *Ladies*, this happen'd above two thousand Years ago, before the Appellation, I now use to you, was known; when Women and Wives, like Horses, and Cows,[24] were call'd by their proper Names; before *Madam* and *Sir* made Parts of civil Speech; long before Quadrille, Dress, Tea and Visits became the whole

---

23 *The Feminiad* (1754), p. 26. "I very much wonder how it came to pass that I did not hear a syllable of Mr Duncombe's performance [*Feminiad*] till Miss Sally [Sally Chapone, daughter of Sarah Chapone, who would probably have known about her mother's anonymous contributions to the *WM*] happened to rumage it out amongst other things for my entertainment that evening which I spent without You at North-End." Thomas Edwards to SR (May 29, 1754), *Correspondence with George Cheyne and Thomas Edwards*, ed. David E. Shuttleton and John A. Dussinger (Cambridge: Cambridge University Press, 2013), p. 326.

24 See footnote 21.

Business of Life; and when the finest of your Sex thought it not beneath them to be good for something.

An eerie anticipation of Margaret Atwood's *The Handmaid's Tale*, this satiric view of woman's subjugation like cattle is the constant refrain in Chapone's attack on marriage lacking a religious basis. An inescapable, if unintended, effect of visualizing such a world is its erotic empowerment of the male over the female body, and it should not come as a surprise that Richardson was inspired to create the story of a master's bondage over a servant girl who refused to surrender her freedom as a sentient being.

An unsigned letter addressed to *Delia, WM,* No. 299 (September 15, 1738), almost certainly by Richardson, praises her response to *Hooker* and urges her to contribute to the *WM*:

> I was so much pleased with the Performance, and so charm'd[25] with the Religious Zeal[26] of its Author, that I immediately determin'd to give the World some Intimation of what it has lost in the Concealment of a Letter[27] adorn'd with such Beauty of Stile and Honesty of Sentiment. No one would have been surpriz'd at its being a Woman's Production, who would have given himself Time to recollect the natural Genius of that Sex, its readiness and expertness to take every thing it is suffer'd to learn.[28] I have often lamented the Disadvantages Ladies lie under in that

---

25 "I am charmed with your Definition of Simplicity; and the Distinction you make in its Favour over Sincerity is worthy of Mrs. Chapone." Carroll, *Selected Letters,* p. 210.

26 "You know him to be a man of probity, of piety. He is a zealous Catholic; and you must allow, that a religious zeal is a strengthener, a confirmer, of all the social sanctions." *Sir Charles Grandison,* 3rd ed. (1754), Vol. 6, p. 90.

27 "You are doubtful with regard to the Women's Genius, 'whether till the World is ended, a Lady is not justified in fearing she should be looked upon like an Owl among the Birds, by the Exertion of it; and should lose more Credit with the Majority, than she can gain with the Few.' Must not the Attempt to mend the World be begun? And how shall it be better begun, in this Instance, than by Conviction arising from the Performances of Women themselves?

Credit with the Majority, my dear Sir!—Who would not prefer to that, a Reputation with the judicious Few? The Opinion of such will in time bring over to them, the Judgment of the Many. But, Sir, can a Woman's Genius, where a fine one, be hidden from the Circle of her Acquaintance?" SR to Thomas Edwards (July 25, 1754), *Correspondence with George Cheyne and Thomas Edwards,* ed. Shuttleton and Dussinger, p. 337.

28 "What a prodigy of learning, in the short reign of Edward the VIth, was the Lady Jane Grey! – Greek, as well as Latin, was familiar to her: So it was to Queen Elizabeth. And can it be supposed, that the natural genius's of those Ladies were more confined,

respect, and how seldom they are permitted any Acquaintance but with the Needle, or Pincushion; or are favour'd with any Communications but from the Governess, or Teacher. In that fine Mould Nature has cast her greatest Delicacies; and tho' thus denied the liberal Improvements of Men, some of them have crept out of their Bounds and Province of Embroidery and Plain-work, and have exhibited ingenious Pieces to entertain the Mind, as well as fine Shaded Works to feast the Sight.

Ironically, while admiring *Delia*'s genius the anonymous writer goes on to extoll the merits of another female author he knows but avoids mentioning by name—*Belinda*. Not surprisingly, Richardson seems to be creating a rivalry between the two "Championesses"![29]

In her response to *Hooker* and *Belinda*, *WM*, No. 304 (October 21, 1738), *Delia* at first playfully pretends to be weak-minded and dependent on male monitors but then challenges her patriarchal authorities:

Mr. *Hooker* and you concur and seem to vie with each other who shall be the most complaisant to us.[30] And therefore, instead of reproaching us with our Faults and Follies, you have with the most refined and delicate kind of Flattery, set before our Eyes this fine Picture, not to shew us what we are, but what we ought to be; and what a Woman of Sense might really be, with a very little.

Instead of being placed on a pedestal, *Delia* protests, a woman should be accepted as an equal companion:

But why a Man with natural Good Sense of his own, improved by a liberal Education; should grudge a Woman the Pleasure of reading any thing besides Books of Cookery, and Receipts in Surgery and Physick, I never could guess.[31] Certainly such a one, however Fair she may be, can be no very agreeable Companion to a Man of Letters.

---

or limited, for their knowledge of Latin and Greek?" *Grandison*, 3rd ed. (1754), Vol. 6, p. 359.
29 "She [Mrs. Chapone] is a great Championess for her Sex." Carroll, *Selected Letters*, p. 340.
30 That is, Richardson and Webster have conspired to set highest standard of womanhood.
31 Same situation as in *WM*, No. 290 (July 14, 1738), on plight of educated wife with boorish husband.

After this letter, a whole year passes before *Belinda* returns to mourn the death of *Delia* and her own confidence as a writer, *WM*, No. 353 (September 29, 1739). A number of questions arise about how these writers decided to abandon the masquerade, beginning with how *Belinda* had reason to believe that *Delia* decided to cease contributing to the *WM*.

> I was made to believe that my former Letters were in some degree of Credit with your Readers, and that *Belinda*, as Times go, was reckon'd a good smart, lively Girl, with some little Humour. Inquiry was made after me, and such as knew, or suspected me to be the Author, congratulated me upon it. This, you may be sure, was pleasing enough to our natural Desire of Praise, and excited an Ambition to add to the Reputation which I had acquired. But two Circumstances unfortunately conspired to check my aspiring Thoughts, and to frustrate my Views. ---- The superior Excellence and Success of a *Rival* is what no Person of any Spirit could ever bear with Temper, and I have been *rival'd* and *excell'd*, not only by one of my own Sex, but by my self. The first requires need not tell you that *Delia* was my *Female* Rival, any more than I can deny the Superiority of her Genius and Performances.

For an author not known for publicizing his inner motives, this confession that he learned from Sarah Chapone's writing about his own defects and subsequently retired to improve himself is most remarkable. Note that this was written near the end of September 1739. By now, something much bigger is in the works than this airy feminist of a journal. Richardson himself claimed November 10, 1739 to January 10, 1739, as the period for the composition of *Pamela, or Virtue Rewarded*. After finding his Belinda was becoming stale, Richardson sought fresh pastures and hit upon a more sustained series of letters by an educated servant girl who conquers a would-be libertine.

Perhaps an important influence during his brief retirement was Aaron Hill, many of whose works he printed. *Belinda's* remarks on composition and style draw a significant comparison to the art of painting:

> I believe, there is nothing more difficult than to write with Accuracy and Elegancy, nothing of which there are fewer good Judges; and yet every one who barely understands the Meaning of the *Words* in which any Book is written will presume, without Examination, to pronounce authoritatively upon its *Defects*, or *Beauties*; which is as great an Absurdity as if an ignorant Clown should attempt to criticize upon the masterly Strokes of a *Raphael*, or a *Titian*; a *Vandyke*, or a *Kneller*.

This failure of the critic to apprehend the unique qualities of artistic genius is echoed in a dialogue presented by Hill:

> What I am angry at, is, that they are admired more for their *Antiquity* than *real Excellence*, by a Set of ignorant Wretches, that, (if I may be allowed the Expression) know only the *Hand-writing* of *Raphael*, *Correggio*, or *Titian*, without being able to taste the Beauties of their *Style*.[32]

It is probably no coincidence that both *Belinda* and Hill cite Raphael and Titian. In *Pamela*, Richardson inserts a poem by Hill that alludes to the same masters:

> *Of all that pleas'd my ravish'd Eye*
> *Her Beauty should supply the Place;*
> *Bold Raphael's Strokes, and* Titian's *Dye,*
> *Should but in vain presume to vye*
> *With her inimitable Face.*[33]

Hill, of course, was one of the first to read this pioneering work and was so effusive with praise that even Richardson tried to restrain him.[34]

Even if we have no evidence that Chapone was corresponding with Richardson at this date, *Delia*'s farewell letter, *WM*, No. 360 (November 17, 1739), indicates that she has paid close attention to *Belinda*'s addresses and emulates her self-abnegating remarks about her writing ability and declines the reputed honor of being her rival. Her opening description of all the paraphernalia from the apothecary caricatures her supposed old age vis-à-vis *Belinda*'s supposed youth: "You, by your own Account, are young, and may hope for the Recovery of your Health, and a long successful Reign."[35] Toward

---

32 *The Prompter* (April 29, 1735). Richardson printed the entire run of this journal, Maslen, p. 30.
33 *Pamela: Or Virtue Rewarded, The Cambridge Edition of the Works of Samuel Richardson*, ed. Albert J. Rivero (Cambridge: Cambridge University Press, 2011), p. 267. "The Messenger," *The Works of Aaron Hill, Esq.* (1753), Vol. I, pp. 155–156.
34 SR wrote a note above a letter from Hill (July 29, 1741: "All Mr Hill's praises too warm, and should be lowered greatly. Yet no Man Ever had a more expanded Heart, and *truer* Friendship, nor more Sincerity." *Correspondence with Aaron Hill and the Hill Family* (The Cambridge Edition of the Correspondence of Samuel Richardson, Series Number 1) (Cambridge: Cambridge University Press, 2013), p. 104.
35 Although only 40 years old at this time, Chapone, like a lot of women in the period, felt the weight of trying to be socially useful after passing the age of childbirth. After reaching age 52 Chapone invokes old age to obviate any romantic love in her effusive

the end of this letter, *Delia* mentions quite specifically various manuscripts she has "upon the Anvil" and leaves no doubt that she is not really finished writing. Shortly after this letter was published, *Pamela, or Virtue Rewarded* appeared, and both *Belinda* and *Delia* departed the stage, never to be mentioned in Richardson's surviving correspondence.

---

expression to Richardson: "As I am an Old Woman, and have never seen you, Sir, I think I may venture to tell you, without being supposed to have in Mind to run away with you, that I am with the most rapid Affection."
[Mrs. Chapone to SR, N. d., but answers his March ?, 1752 and answered (after a delay) April 18, *FM XII*, 2, *ff.*]

Chapter 4

SELECTED TEXTS OF *THE WEEKLY MISCELLANY*

1. *Weekly Miscellany*, No. XXVII (27). Saturday, June 16, 1733

I hope I shall be excus'd for postponing several excellent Letters, while I entertain my Readers with a pleasant one from a young Lady. As it is the first which have received from the Sex, I could do no less than give it a Preference, tho' some may be of Opinion that I should have consulted my own Credit better by not publishing it at all. If the Lady intended it only as a private Admonition, she should have given me some Intimation of her Meaning, but as it came without any Injunction of Secrecy, I thought myself at Liberty to make my own Use of it. The Ingenuity of it, I dare say, will make it agreeable to the Publick; and the good Humour of it cannot fail of making it inoffensive to the *old Lady* and the *Curate* who, next to *myself*, are most affected by the seeming Severity of her Banter. I shall give it exactly as it came to me.

To Richard Hooker, *Esq;*

SIR,

I cannot say that I am ever *a Reader,* or often an *Admirer,* but it is my Misfortune that I am always *a Hearer,* of your *Miscellany.* I live with an old Maiden Aunt, who mightily likes the Piety of your Design, and the Gravity of your Performances. She longs for the coming in of the Post with as much Impatience as I should expect a Letter from my Lover. As soon as the Letter-Carrier knocks at the Door (which is generally in the Evening) the Candles, the Curate, and Miss are call'd for in great haste. When the good old Gentlewoman has properly placed a little Instrument to her Ear, and the Reverend Gentleman has fixed another upon his Nose, your dry Discourse is bawled out with a Voice as loud as would reach the largest Church in your City, and in a Tone as canting as any that was in Fashion in the Times of old *Noll*.¹ If any Part be duller; I ask your Pardon, good Sir, I mean graver, than ordinary, it is sure to strike their Want of Fancy, and we must needs have it over again. I shall dread the Sound of *Encore* as much as a dying Wretch trembles at the Toll of his passing Bell.² If you have any Humour in you (and if you have, why are you so sparing of it when it is so much wanted?) forbear smiling, if you can, when you imagine to yourself what an odd Groupe [*sic*] of Figures we make. There is a Painter, as I have been told, in Covent-Garden, who excels in humourous Pieces, and never fails to crowd a Parson into ridiculous Company; if he will come down and draw us as he finds us, without giving himself the Trouble of Invention, he may make a very entertaining Picture of us. He will see one Figure in the Corner of the Room, which will very much heighten the Ridicule, and give Life to the whole Piece, tho' he places himself in such Obscurity. You must know the Justice's eldest Son is an humble Servant of mine; and as many a gay young Fellow has frequented a Conventicle to worship his Mistress, instead of his Maker, this polite Gentleman puts himself to the Mortification of attending your Saturday's Lecture, in Hopes of gaining my Aunt's Consent by complimenting her Judgment: And he does not shew more Artifice by his constant Attendance, than by the Choice of his Situation; where he has an Opportunity of shewing his Wit, after the Dutch Manner, by strange Grimaces and antick Gestures.³ While he passes, with my Aunt, for a sober, hopeful young Man, he is the veriest Wag in Nature, and can make a Jest of what he does not understand, as well as the toppingest Wit that ever embellished the Outside of his Head. I cannot say but the Creature diverts me, but then he distresses me too; for, as it is generally my Office to hold the Candle **[middle column]** to the Doctor, and so am placed in full View, I am forced to put myself to Pain for fear of giving Offence, and bite my Lip that I may keep my Countenance. Now, good Mr. Hooker, as my Spark and I are oblig'd to be your constant Auditors, I hope you are so much a Gentleman, that you will now and then give us something that is fit for Gentlemen and Ladies to hear. You may write as many Papers as you will upon Test Acts, provided you will sometimes give us a Test of your Wit and Pleasantry. If you talk to your learned Readers, concerning deep Points in moral Philosophy, why must not we in our Turn, have a lively Essay, which will be more entertaining, and not inconsistent with your declared Design? You have made a great Rout

---

1 Nickname for Oliver Cromwell (1599–1658), military leader and Lord Protector 1653-58 after the Civil War.
2 Church bells rung to announce the death of a parishioner.
3 See footnote 24.

about the Genuineness of an old History; but what is it to us who was the Author of a Book, which we never intend to read? You have put yourself into some Heat about People's not going to Church; but, I assure you, we go twice every Sunday, and are no ways concerned in those pathetick Exhortations. In short, we should be as much diverted, and perhaps as much edified, if a small Portion of Greek were to be read to us, and my Beau would have the same Conveniency of cracking his bodily Jokes in the Corner. I must therefore take the honest Freedom to tell you, if you write to the Publick, you must a little consult the Taste of the Publick, or your Lectures will stand a bad Chance, either to lie peaceably at the Publisher's, or to rest as peaceably upon the Table.[4] Besides, how can you expect to do us any Good, unless you give us a good Opinion of yourself? But if you go on at this unmerciful Rate, we shall take you for some Testy old Batchelor, whose Discourses partake of the Sowerness of his Spirits; and that you publish your Instructions only to gratify your Spleen. Harkee, 'Squire; Can you take Advice, as well as give it? Be not more nice than wise. A very wise Man has told me that there is a Time for all Things. Be sometimes merry, and you shall have for your Friend

Northamptonshire.
BELINDA.

It was the Observation of a very eminent Physician, that if the World did but talk of him, he did not care what they said of him.[5] If we understand this Maxim, as it ought to be understood, to relate to his Eminence and Success in his Profession, there is a great deal of good Sense in it, tho' some Allowance must be made for the Strength of the Expression. I am so far of his Opinion, that I am pleased with the Letter from *Belinda,* tho' I should have been much better pleas'd if it had been a Letter of Thanks. Her Approbation would have done me publick Honour; but the greatest Disgrace is to be thought below Notice. It is an Argument of some Merit that she will correspond with me; for, if her Reproof shews that I deserve Correction, it is also a Sign that she does not think me incapable of Amendment. As I shall endeavour to make a proper Use of her Suggestions, I shall return some Part of her Freedom by letting her know that she mistakes the Design of the *Miscellany,* if she thinks it was intended chiefly for Amusement. I am the more inclined to think she may be under this mistaken Apprehension, because an Author who undertook to give an Account of our Paper, observed that we formed it upon the Plan of the

---

4 Richardson the printer giving advice about circulation of the journal.
5 Possibly George Cheyne (1671–1743), Scottish physician and friend of Richardson.

Tatlers and *Spectators*. As I apprehend, the principal Aim of those inimitable Essays was to divert Mankind, and correct those little Foibles which had not been distinctly considered by Moralists, and were below the Animadversions of the Pulpit; tho' it must be owned, that they sometimes rose up to Subjects of the most important Nature. Agreeably to this Design, Wit and Humour, Pleasantry and Ridicule, were with great Advantage employed to make Men ashamed of Folly and Vanity; and even where they expos'd **[right column]** real Vices, they shewed the Absurdity and Weakness, rather than the sinful Nature of the Action. The primary End of the *Miscellany* is to guard the Minds of the People against the Attempts of Infidels to introduce an universal Irreligion and Immorality; and to defend the Church of *England* against the united Efforts of Infidels and Sectaries to destroy it; tho' we shall descend, when more important Points do not demand our immediate Consideration, to Things of a lighter Kind. In a Design therefore where Truth is to be set in a clear Light by the Evidence of Reason, and Sophistry to be detected by accurate Distinctions; where Falshoods and Misrepresentations of Facts are to be exposed by the Authority of History; in such Cases there does not seem to be much Room for Wit and Humour to exercise their proper Function. I have acknowledged that Wit is one of the noblest Faculties of the human Mind, and has been successfully employed on the most serious Occasions, by the most serious, even inspired, Writers; yet, it must be allowed, that some Subjects are not so naturally fit to be treated in the ludicrous Way, and that few Writers are qualified with Talents of so exquisite and delicate a Kind, while many are capable of arguing in a clear, strong, and agreeable Manner. I could name many Authors of our own Age and Nation who are undeniable Examples of the Force of Wit, when properly applied; and I wish they would, on this Occasion, give fresh Instances of its great Use. But must no Man undertake the Cause of God and his Country, against the common Enemies of both, unless he is blessed with the superior Genius of a *Swift*, a *Pope*, or an *Arbuthnot*?[6] Or can no Man expect to please, unless he makes his Reader laugh? Good Sense, expressed in significant Terms, and in a spirited Style, will always be agreeable to a good Understanding, where the Mind does not bring strong Prejudices against the Subject Matter of the Discourse. Whoever has a bad Head, or a bad Heart, we can neither write to the Capacity, nor intend to write to the Taste, of such a Reader; but as *Belinda* does not want Apprehension, and discovers no Disrelish for Religion and Virtue, I do not despair of having her for one of my Friends who will oblige others, as well as

---

6 *Hooker*'s remarkable canonization of these three satirists may imply Richardson's own ambition to emulate their masterful irony.

his Worship's Heir, to attend to our Lectures. The Raillery of her Letter I consider as an Exercise of her Imagination, not the Effect of a real Dislike. If the *Miscellany* has suffered in her Opinion by the Disadvantage of a disagreeable Voice and Accent, I desire for the future, that the Curate and *Belinda* may exchange Offices. By the Help of her Instrument the old Gentlewoman may hear her, tho' she may not be able to speak so loud; and if *Belinda's* Person be as agreeable as her Mind, the Curate will be as well pleased to hold the Candle, and have no Occasion for his Spectacles. After all, if this Lady will promise never to read any immoral Books or Pamphlets, and to silence her *Spark*, if he offers in her Company to advance any Deistical or profane Notions, I will intercede with her Aunt that she may not be obliged any more to hear the *Miscellany*. Yet I cannot but commend the old Lady for taking some Care to secure those under her Authority from the Plague of Infidelity, which at present is very rife in this Kingdom, and destroys Numbers of innocent young People; and if every House were provided with some such Weekly Antidote, Fathers and Masters would soon find the salutary Effects of it, in the Dispositions and Manners of their Children and Servants; from whence the Interest, the Comfort, and Happiness of private Life must be derived.

I am obliged to *Belinda* for reminding me, that Good nature and Benevolence in a Writer will be of the greatest Force to recommend his Writings, be they of what Kind they will, and that the finest Compositions will be disgustful and ineffectual, as to any good Influence on the Reader, when an Author **[next page]** writes, not that he may do good to others by his Instructions, but to ease himself by discharging a proper Quantity of Gall and Ire.

I am very sensible too, that a chearful Writer, like a chearful Companion, will always be most acceptable; but, as the Lady very well observes from the best Authority, there is a Time for all Things. The Author whom she has quoted says farther, that *Mirth does Good like a Medicine*; but he has also observed, unluckily enough for your over-merry People, that *much Laughter is a Sign of great Folly.*[7] In Exchange therefore for her Piece of Proverbial Advice, I shall make her a Present of another, equally useful and seasonable, viz. *That she would be merry and wise.* To be pleased with humourous Compositions, when **[middle column]** the Humour is well applied, and well regulated, is a Proof of Taste; but an Incapacity to be pleas'd, unless an Author keeps his *Reader* all the while upon the Titter and the Grin, is an Argument of senseless Levity. If *Belinda* will be a good Girl, she shall now and then have a short Essay, that may improve her Understanding without giving her the

---

7 *Proverbs* 17: 22.

Trouble of much Thought; and sometimes a little Poetry that will entertain her Imagination, without corrupting her Heart.

R. H.

Before I receive any more Obligations, it will be some Pleasure to me to acknowledge those which I have already received. For several Letters and **[right column]** Poems, which have given great Satisfaction, I am indebted to particular Friends whom I can thank in private. But I am obliged to two Gentlemen who are wholly *unknown* to me, and likely to continue so, because I have not the Liberty to enquire who they are. One of them has sent me several agreeable Things under the Name of *Eusebius*, which shew him to be a Gentleman of Humanity, good Sense, and a polite Taste. The other, by his Correspondence Abroad, has furnished me with an Opportunity of enriching the *Miscellany* with the *Literary Articles*. As I have no other Method of doing it, I hope these Gentlemen will not be offended with this grateful Acknowledgement of their Kindness.

2. *Weekly Miscellany*, No. XLII (42). Saturday, September 29, 1733

To Mr. Hooker.

I am obliged to be your Monitor again. Remember the Title of your Paper, and keep up to it. You have of late been very indulgent to the Serious, and it is Time you say something to the gay Part of your Readers. If we young Folks can have Patience to attend to so many grave Lectures, such as are old either in Constitution or Temper, must excuse you if you apply yourself sometimes to our Imagination, by sprightly and humourous Compositions. When the Solemn and the Demure take such Offence at innocent Amusement, I cannot help thinking that Envy is at the Bottom of their Displeasure. Through the Decay or Heaviness of their Spirits, they have no Relish for Strokes of Fancy, or Turns of Wit, and then their Want of Taste must be dignified with the Character of Wisdom. But be that as it will, we expect to be consider'd as well as they; or we shall resent it as strongly. If you insert this, you shall hear from

Belinda.

I am very glad that I have it in my Power to oblige my fair Correspondent without any Danger of disobliging the very gravest Part of my Readers: I shall say nothing more in Behalf of a Performance which will speak for itself, nor detain them from a greater Pleasure, than I can give them by an Encomium upon the Poem.

Poem: "A Letter to a Friend on the Death of his Cow."

First advertisement of *The Apprentice's Vade Mecum*, repeated continually in later issues.

3. *Weekly Miscellany*, No. LIII (53). Saturday, December 15, 1733.

Letter from Belinda.

To Mr. HOOKER.

Alas, poor Gentleman! I am sorry to hear you talk of *Stopping Payment*. I have indeed been in Pain for you some time, and out of pure Compassion avoided importuning you for the little Matter you owe me. You have found out an ingenious Way of turning your Debts over to others, and if you can but perswade People to pay them for you, I shall be as well satisfied.[8] You own, your Proposals gave the Publick reason to expect some *Wit*, but it seems they were not intended as an absolute *Promise,* but an *Invitation* to the *Wits* of *Great-Britain* to shew their Parts. With all my Heart. But what say you to the Letter you wrote me in one of your former *Miscellanies*? I really took it for a Promise, but if you meant only to *invite* me to relieve you in your Distress, I am ready to do it to the utmost of my Power. I had you in my Thoughts before you made your Case known, and endeavour'd to raise a *Collection* for you. I met with several *well dispos'd Christians,* but no great *Wits*. The *Curate* in particular expressed a very tender Sense of your Condition, but modestly pleaded, that his Genius does not lie that Way. I am afraid your Readers will be of Opinion, that I have mistaken my *own* Capacity, how justly soever I may judge of other People's. Yet, I shall attempt to give you some Account of the present State of *Wit* in *our* Parts, and risque the Credit of my Discretion for the Pleasure of indulging my Generosity.

In my first Letter I told you of a *Spark* that has a Month's Mind[9] to me, and takes great Pains to recommend himself to my Favour. This hopeful Youth may *literally* be said to have all their Venom collected in a little *Sting,* Vipers

---

8 *Belinda*'s figurative economics barely disguises the fact that Webster was financially indebted to his well-intentioned printer.

9 "Chiefly *Roman Catholic Church*. The commemoration of a deceased person by the celebration of a requiem mass, prayers, etc., on a day one month from the date of the death or funeral." *OED*. Perhaps *Belinda* is implying that such dangerous libertines can be the cause of death for a virtuous woman.

and Adders in a small *Bag* in their *Gam*.¹⁰ The *Cunning* of your *Sex is said to lie all in your* Eye Teeth, and you may have heard of the great Virtue of a *Colt's Tooth:* the *Archness* of my *Squire* is contained in the Compass of a *Forefinger.* When he gets snug in the Corner behind my Aunt, the Body being duly disposed, he gently touches the Extremity of one Side of his Nose with the *End* of the said Finger, and immediately it gives a *witty* Cast to every Feature, puts all the Muscles into a humourous Motion, and **[middle column]** makes him all over so very a *Wag*,¹¹ he hardly retains the Figure of a *Man*. If you kept a Stage, he might be of Use to you, and I would lay my Commands upon him; but this kind of Wit being to be *seen*, and not *read*, I shall keep him here for my own Diversion on a rainy Day, or in a Fit of the Vapours.¹²

We have likewise in this Country, purely of our own Growth and Education, an inferior Sort of these *sensible* Wits, who can do nothing with a *single Figure*, but have a great deal of *Waggery* in their *whole Fist*, especially if it be a *heavy* one: And, if you allow them the Use of *both* Hands, they can be intolerably Witty, *make you split your Sides* with Laughing; unless you happen to be the *Subject* of their Wit, and then it is as much as can be expected if you laugh only on *one Side of your Mouth*. The Way of *Silencing* these Jokers¹³ when they grow too Severe, is, by fastening them to their Chairs, or tying their Hands. I cannot conveniently send you a *Collection* of this sort of Wit, neither can we

---

10 Teeth. *OED*.
11 "A mischievous boy (often as a mother's term of endearment to a baby boy); in wider application, a youth, young man, a 'fellow', 'chap'. Obsolete." *OED*. Richardson uses this term to describe a crafty manipulator:

"The Occasion was owing to the frequent Slights I had received from the Gentlewoman with whom I lodge, and from others of my Friends, who, believing that I lived up to my scanty Fortune, as in Truth I do (tho' I take care to be beholden to nobody, and pay ready Money for every thing), could not treat me negligently enough. I complain'd of this to that arch Wag *Tony Richards*, who told me he would change every one's Behaviour to me in a few Days. And he has done it effectually: For what does he do, but, as a kind of Secret, acquaints my Landlady, that beside my poor little Estate (which you know to be my All) he had lately discovered, that I had twenty thousand Pounds Stock in one of our great Companies!"

Such was the Force of his whimsical Delusion, that, the very next Morning, I had a clean Towel hung over my Water-bottle, tho' I never before had more than one a Week during the twenty Years I have lodged here." Letter CLXIII, *Familiar Letters* (1750), p. 259.
12 " 3.b.1662–A morbid condition supposed to be caused by the presence of such exhalations; depression of spirits, hypochondria, hysteria, or other nervous disorder. Now *archaic*. (Common *c*1665–1750.)" *OED*.
13 In the Chadwyck-Healy *ECF* database, the term *joker* occurs once in *Pamela* and four times in *Grandison*. The only two other occurrences are in *Peregrine Pickle*.

spare any of it at this Season, but if you'll make my Aunt (who receives People of your Condition very civilly) a Visit in the Holidays, you shall see some of it.

You must understand, Mr. *Hooker,* that my Aunt having a Desire that I should know something more of the Matter than the Generality of my Sex; we are at present in a Course of *Philosophical Lectures,* and last Night the *Curate* (who is our *Tutor*) read a Chapter out of one *Lock,* upon Human Understanding, where the Author talks of a *Scale* of Beings.[14] His Terms being a little awkward to me as yet, I did not very well understand him, but I fancy he means something like what I have observed in the *different Kinds of Wits* rising above one another by almost imperceptible *Degrees,* or *Steps.* The Wag who is witty with *both* Hands comes but little short of him who can do the Business with *one*; and the *one-handed* Wit falls but little below the *Squire* who performs Wonders with his *Finger.* I have consider'd this curious Point so nicely as to be able to determine in what *Rank* to place the *Shrug,* the *Grin,* the *Leer,* and the *Wink*; and therefore I shall pass on to the next Class of Wits amongst us, which cannot be called *Bodily* Wits; because they carry about them some *real* Wit, tho' it be none of their own.

The lowest of this Class is poor *Poll,*[15] who is now leaning her Ear towards me with *arch* Attention. *Poll* has all the Wit that is stirring in the Family, or in the Neighbourhood of the Window where she takes the Air in fine Weather; and, like most other Wits, she has a strange Fondness for *naughty Expressions,* and *paw Words.*[16] She abuses civil People as they go along the Streets, and puts us Maidens to the Blush. Because we talk freely among ourselves, and now and then say a merry Thing, without meaning any Hurt, this indiscreet Creature (for Wit and Judgment ever are at Strife) blabs it all out when you filthy Men are with us. I could have killed her the other Day for saying, I know what, before a *Toupee,* who will never let us hear the last

---

14 *Belinda* may be referring to Book II of Locke's *Essay*: Chapter 28 discusses ideas of moral relations. See Fraser edition (New York: Dover, 1959), Vol. II, pp. 473–485. But the phrase "scale of beings' is not found in Locke. It comes close to the neoPlatonic "great chain of Being" alluded to in Pope's *An Essay on Man,*" I. l. 33. See the Twickenham Edition, III.i. ed. Maynard Mack (London: Methuen, 1950). At this time Richardson was printing Locke's *The Reasonableness of Christianity, as delivered in the Scriptures* (1731; 1736). Maslen, pp. 446–447. After her marriage Pamela was a keen advocate of Locke's treatise on the education of children, and Richardson's protégée Sarah Wescomb used it as her guide when becoming a mother. See Lady Scudamore to SR (March 12, 1758), *The Cambridge Edition of the Correspondence of Samuel Richardson: Correspondence with Sarah Wescomb, Frances Grainger, and Laetitia Pilkington,* ed. Dussinger, p. 253.
15 "A conventional proper or pet name for a parrot. Hence: a parrot. Cf. Polly n." *OED*.
16 "Improper, obscene. Chiefly in paw word. Cf. paw-paw *adj.* "*OED*.

of it. When she's in high Humour, the favourite Joke is, in a *drawling* Way, to cry *Parson*, and then set up a loud Laugh. But we were most surpriz'd at some Words which she seems to have taken a particular Fancy to; *Relations, Fitnesses, Nature,* &c. Upon asking the *Curate* what might be the Meaning of this Language, he assured us, that it is the common Cant of *Freethinkers*. This put us upon enquiring, of the *Squire*, who made us a Present of the Bird, after her *Education* and *Acquaintance*, and I find she was brought up at a famous *Coffee-House* near the *Temple*, where the *smartest Wits* and the *ablest Freethinkers* resort. In short, *Poll* is so exceedingly *Polite*, my Aunt has given **[right column]** her Warning; upon which the *Squire* (if I'll give him Leave) proposes to introduce her into the Acquaintance of some *great Folks*, in hopes of advancing *himself* as well as *Poll*.

Next above *Poll*, rises a vast Body of Wits, differing rather in a small Degree of *Perfection*, than in *Kind*. These, like *Poll*, treasure up as much of what they apprehend to be *Wit*, as their *Memory* will hold, which they dispose of as freely, and generally, with as much Discretion. But as they are not confin'd to a *Cage*, but can go into a Variety of Company, it must be owned they have, many of them, a good deal more Wit than the *Bird*. Our Country, as well as others, has the Honour of giving Birth to many of these Genius's; but *London* has the Credit of making *Wits* of them. A Party of them came down here last Vacation, and several of our innocent Country Girls thought as well of *them* as they did of *themselves*; but I dare swear, all their Jokes were as old as *Infidelity, Prophaneness,* and *Obscenity*. As to the great Quantity of Darts and Flames, the Sun, Moon and Stars, Angels, and a great deal more, which were all at my Service; they were stollen [sic] from the *Playhouses*, where these Gallants furnish themselves with Sets of Compliments.

But in Justice to our Country, I must tell you, it produces something above *Harlequins* and *Parrots*. We have two young Gentlemen (which, as Times go, are a great many) in this Neighbourhood, who are small *Authors*. They are both of them as industrious as the merry Mortal in the Corner, to be well with me, and I have condescended to make it my Request that they would write something for the *Miscellany*; and I thought they would do their best, because I am your constant Reader, or Hearer. But, to my very great Surprize, they have *implored* me to think of some other, *any* other Commands; representing, that they have some *Credit* and some *Interest* in the World, and that I should make a most tyrannical Use of my Power, if I made the Loss of their *Reputation*, and all *Expectations in Life*, the Condition of my Favour; adding further, that they could have no Hopes of continuing long in my Esteem, when they were become *ridiculous* to the rest of the World. Without giving any Answer to so strange a Speech, I ordered them to withdraw, that I might take Time to consider of it; and I have taken so much Time, I have never seen them since.

I had still some Hopes from a good *smart Divine*; who sometimes gives the Curate a Sermon, that my Aunt may invite him afterwards to Dinner. He always calls for your Paper, and says handsome Things of it. I thought, considering the Gravity of his Profession, it would come better from my *Aunt* than from a young Girl, and so I put her upon asking the Doctor to give us a Letter upon the *Saturday*, as well as a Sermon upon the *Sunday*; and I took the Liberty of desiring that his Letter might neither be so *grave*, nor so *long*, as his Sermon. The good Man, you may be sure, was full of Bows and Compliments, and Speeches about the *Goodness* of the Design, and his *violent* Inclination to promote it, but said, that it was generally *Preaching*, and the World was tired with Preaching already; that there were Principles, however true, advanced in it that are not so acceptable to many People, and that he could not tell how such a publick Encouragement of the Paper *might be taken*. Without any Ceremony my Aunt told him, she was afraid he would be in the Dark, and called for his Horse.

I think, Mr. *Hooker*, I have been very kind to you, and in return I expect to hear what *Sorts* and *Degrees* of Wits you have in *London*; for if the *Parcel* you lately sent us, be a Sample of your very *best* Sort, I stand a bad Chance for a good Husband, and an agreeable Companion.

Northamptonshire. BELINDA.

You know a Woman seldom writes a Letter without a Postscript, and I forgot to tell you, you may soon expect something in the *grave* Way from hence. The *Curate* and *my Aunt* have been laying their Heads together, and I accidentally saw a great Heap of Blots and Blurs with your Name in Front.

If an unlucky Story, about *Fleet Ditch*,[17] does not put off our Journey, we are to be in *London* about the meeting of the Parliament,[18] and I am forming *great Designs for the Service of your Paper*.

I have observ'd that you distinguish several Words by a particular Character; if you meet with any in my Letter that merit Distinction, pray do them Justice.

Where you see Occasion, correct me as severely as you please.

---

17 Fleet Ditch, a slum area with underground sewer that had treacherous mud.
18 At the time Parliament opens for the session.

4. *Weekly Miscellany*, No. CXXXII (132). Saturday, June 28, 1735

To the Author of the Weekly Miscellany.

Sir,

The Cause in which you are engaged, may at first View, appear too weighty to receive Assistance from the weak Arm of *Woman*. We are generally esteemed incapable of *Reason* and *Argument*, and, I dare say, the *Free-thinkers* of the Age ascribe it entirely to this, that we are still so fond of *Churches* and *Prayer-Books*, and can sit with Patience once or twice a Week, to hear a formal Parson harangueing upon *Morality* and *Religion*. But 'tis their Fate to be mistaken in this, as it is in almost every thing else: Our Religion is not the Effect of less Understanding but of our having more Modesty than the other Sex; and they might as well ascribe to the Superiority of their Reason, Drinking, Swearing, and other such valuable Prerogatives which they claim as the Birth-right of their Sex. For us, we confess we have not such Strength of Parts as to be above Shame; we should as much avoid visiting or conversing with an *Infidel* in *Petticoats*, as with a common Prostitute. It is very fortunate, **[next page]** that it is still quite scandalous for a *Woman* to be vicious; even the worst of your Sex are seldom pleased with their own Vices in ours; the greatest Sot would abhor a drunken Wife; and I'm very much mistaken, if a *Deist* or *Infidel* would like one that is no Christian, they being conscious what little Security they could have, for her Person or Inclinations, from any Principles they could afford her: We are therefore in much less Danger of having our Religion corrupted, than the other Sex: But I think it not sufficient for us barely to act upon the defensive, and to preserve ourselves from Danger, but 'tis our Duty to endeavour to rescue others. In order therefore to engage in your Assistance some abler Pens of my own Sex, I shall endeavour to shew, that the Capacities of the *Females* in general, are, in a very peculiar Manner, fitted and adapted to engage and foil the Infidel Party.

The few Authors I have met with in my little Reading, who have writ seriously upon the Faculties of the *Male* and *Female* Understanding, have treated them as one and the same, and ascribe the Superiority of the former barely to the Difference of Education.

Our Souls no Sexes have, their Love is clean,
No Sex—both in the better Part are Men;

Says the witty Sir *Thomas Overbury*.[19] The grave Mr. *Collier* gives it as his Opinion, "That they are mistaken, who imagine that Men have a Superiority by Birth and native Advantage."[20]— And the late ingenious Author of a Pamphlet entitled, *The Hardships of the* English *Laws in Relation to Wives,* is of the same Opinion, and gives this Reason for it; 'That tho' indeed Men, having the Advantages of *Universities, publick Negociations,* and a free unconstrained Converse with Mankind, are generally superior; yet if we consider the Abilities of each Sex antecedently to these Advantages, by looking amongst the vulgar unlearned People, we shall not find in Fact that Men are so much wiser than Women, as to induce us to suppose that their natural Endowments are much greater"—This Author first strengthens her Assertion, by the concurrent Opinions of three of the first Rank in the Republick of Letters *viz.* Mr. *Hobbs,*[21] Mr. *Woolaston,*[22] and the Author of *Revelation examined with Candour;*[23] who, however different in their Sentiments in general, seem to agree in this. From hence she produces an exceeding good Argument for the *Truth of Revelation.* For since the Capacities of one Sex are not naturally greater than the other, there can be no possible Reason assigned for that great Superiority, which the Opinions and Customs of all Nations have given to the *Man,* but that they all had some Footsteps of the original Curse of *Subjection* passed upon the Woman. An Argument which I dare say may defy the Reach and Subtilty of a *Deist* or *Free-thinker.* But tho' I entirely agree that the *Light of Nature* does not in the least prescribe, or even suggest, that great Prerogative over the Wife, which almost every Nation has given him, and consequently, that we must fly to *Scripture* for the Origin of it; yet I in some measure, differ from this Author, and from all the great Names above mentioned. I believe there is a Sort of *Sex* even in the Mind: As much as I can observe of the Works of Nature, she generally forms a Similitude between the Soul and Body to which it is united. This is very easily seen in different Nations. The gay, dancing, feathered, fluttering Race of *France,* are as volatile in their Notions, as in their Legs and Arms; whilst the heavy, plodding, poring *Dutchman* gains his Knowledge, as

---

19 Thomas Overbury (1581–1613), poet, and murdered in the Tower. Quotation from *The Wife, Express'd in a Compleat Wife.*
20 Jeremy Collier (1650–1726), *A Short View of the Immorality and Profaneness of the English Stage* (1698).
21 Thomas Hobbes (1558–1679). English philosopher, author of *Leviathan* (1651), which sets forth a theory of social contract.
22 William Woolaston (1659–1724), English philosopher who advocated theory of Deism.
23 Patrick Delany (1686–1768), Irish clergyman. This book (1732) was printed multiple times by Richardson. See Maslen, pp. 228–235.

he does all his other Riches, by the Dint of Labour and Industry.[24] If different Nations thus differ from each other in the Faculties of their Minds, as well as their Bodies, it seems very probable, that nature has formed at least as much Difference between the Minds of the different Sexes; and this, I believe, will be confirmed by common Experience. *Resolution* and *Fortitude* are usually esteemed *Male* Virtues, and are the proper Companions of *Strength*; as *Compassion* and *Tenderness* are of *Beauty*. Thus with regard to other Faculties; If the Male excels in Depth of Thought and Solidity of Judgment, the Female certainly does as much in Quickness of Apprehension, and Sprightliness of Wit; the former is proper to labour in the Mine, the latter to polish and refine the Ore; Judgment may be the Bones and Sinews of Science; Wit as it were the Animal Spirits. The female Endowments therefore cannot properly be said to be less than the Male, but they are not of the same *Kind;* their Difference does not consist in *Degree,* but in *Nature* and *Quality*.

I fancy your Readers will be apt to imagine, that I have given a Proof against my own Hypothesis by the Heaviness and Dullness of my own Writing, but I think it a true Account of the Qualifications of my Sex in general, how small a Share soever I enjoy of them myself. If you, Mr. *Hooker,* agree with me in this, I dare say you will allow, that the present Set of *Rakes* and *Infidels* have undertaken a Task, for which they are very ill qualified by Nature; a Province which our Sex would shine in much more than they, if we could, like them discard our Consciences, and ruin our Reputations and our Souls, for the poor Renown of being smart and witty. But I hope we shall make that use of our Talents for which God has endued us with them, *viz.* to defend and illustrate, not to oppose and ridicule the Truth. The unknown Author of the pamphlet above mentioned has abundantly shewn, that the gayest Sentiments and liveliest Expressions are not inconsistent with sincere Piety and solid good Sense.

I have the Happiness of knowing several Ladies, who, I'm sure, can exert the same Talents, and give you very great Assistance, if you can engage them in a Correspondence. They will probably not interfere in your Disputes with the *Dissenters,* where Depth of Reading, and great Knowledge of Antiquity, are required; but as to the *Infidel* Tribe, they quitted their Reason when they

---

24 "*Miss Byron, To Miss Selby. Colnebrooke, Sunday Evening.* "Captain Salmonet, she says, appeared to her in a middle way between a French beau and a Dutch boor; aiming at gentility, with a person and shape uncommonly clumsy." *Sir Charles Grandison,* 3rd ed. (1754), Letter V, Vol. 3, p. 30. Mrs. Delany was probably an influence on Richardson's caricatures of foreign stereotypes.

quitted their Religion, and may possibly be bantered, but cannot be argued, into Sense and Good-manners,

I am, Sir,
Your most obedient Servant,

ASPASIA[25]

. . . .

[signed] Aspasia

5. *Weekly Miscellany*, No. CLXXX (180). Saturday, May 29, 1736.

Belinda *is pleased to be very merry with an old Man, but since she is innocently so, I am willing to divert my Readers, tho' the Laugh be at*
Her Obliged Humble Servant,
R. HOOKER.

To 'Squire HOOKER.

SIR,

It is almost two Years since I did you the Favour of writing to you last, and I had laid aside the Thoughts of writing to you any more. I was credibly informed, that *Curiosity,* often fatal to *our* Sex, had occasioned great Enquiry to be made, all over the County of *Northamptonshire,* after the Person of *Belinda.* I cannot say but that I have so much of the *Woman* in me, as to be pleased with Admiration and Applause, even from those whom I despise; and the Merit of doing Justice to *my Wit,* inclin'd me very strongly to return the Compliment, by allowing *them* the Credit of some *Judgment,* tho I know they did not speak their own Sentiments, but the Report of others. My Groupe [*sic*] of *Country Wits,* which I sent you, has procur'd me Abundance of *Country Fools* and *Coxcombs* for my Admirers. 'Squire *Shallow* of — — lately come to a fine Estate, was pleased to *swear* I was a very *smart Girl,* drank a large Bumper to my Health, threw the Glass most gallantly over his Head; then *swore* again, by

---

25 *Aspasia* was Mary Granville's pen name in her correspondence with the Gloucestershire circle.

all that is *good* and *bad,* that he would marry me without a Groat,[26] if he could tell who I was. The poor 'Squire laugh'd heartily at the Picture, little suspecting that he was the capital Figure in it. *Timothy Froth,* Esq; of your House, had express'd some Thoughts of *trying* to find me out, and bestowing himself upon me, to the great Mortification of several young Ladies, who had conceived Hopes of gaining the *great Prize* in the Matrimonial Lottery. Mr. *Shallow's* Estate has no great Charms in *my* Eyes, who have consider'd, a little more than *our* Sex generally do, whence *rational* Happiness arises; and as to Mr. *Froth,* I have naturally so great an Antipathy to *Froth* of all Kinds, that I am ready to swoon at the Sight of *Whipt Syllabub,*[27] or any Thing of that *delicate* Texture. The Compass of your Paper would hardly contain a *Catalogue* of those *worthy* Gentlemen who have said civil Things of *my* Performance, and discover'd great Inclinations to be better acquainted with me. I was thinking with myself one Day, what a *vast Fortune* I could have made myself, if I had declar'd publickly in the *Northampton Mercury,* that I would be *raffled* for, by

---

26 "*Historical.* A denomination of coin (in medieval Latin *grossus,* French *gros,* Italian *grosso,* Middle Dutch *groot*) which was recognized from the 13th cent. in various countries of Europe. Its standard seems to have been in the 14th cent. theoretically one-eighth of an ounce of silver; but its actual intrinsic value varied greatly in different countries and at different periods. (The adoption of the Dutch or Flemish form of the word into English shows that the 'groat' of the Low Countries had circulated here before a coin of that denomination was issued by the English sovereigns.) †a shilling, pound of groats: a Flemish money of account bearing the same proportion to the ordinary 'shilling' or 'pound' as the groat or 'thick penny' did to the ordinary penny." *OED.*

27 Richardson associated this delicacy with French effeminacy. In the prefatory advertisements to the first edition of *Pamela* he includes an anonymous letter from *WM,* No. 407 (October 11, 1740):

"I can't conceive why you should hesitate a Moment as to the Publication of this very natural and uncommon Piece. I could wish to see it out in its own native Simplicity, which will affect and please the Reader beyond all the Strokes of Oratory in the World; for those will but spoil it: and, should you permit such a murdering Hand to be laid upon it, to gloss and tinge it over with superfluous and needless Decorations, which, like too [Page xiii] much Drapery in Sculpture and Statuary, will but incumber it; it may disguise the Facts, marr the Reflections, and unnaturalize the Incidents, so as to be lost in a Multiplicity of fine idle Words and Phrases, and reduce our Sterling Substance into an empty Shadow, or rather *frenchify* our *English* Solidity into Froth and Whip-syllabub. No; let us have *Pamela* as *Pamela* wrote it; in her own Words, without Amputation, or Addition. Produce her to us in her neat Country Apparel, such as she appear'd in, on her intended Departure to her Parents; for such best becomes her Innocence and beautiful Simplicity. Such a Dress will best edify and entertain. The flowing Robes of Oratory may indeed amuse and amaze, but will never strike the Mind with solid Attention."

Although sometimes attributed to Webster, it is also possible that SR himself wrote this advertisement. It surely resembles his style.

twenty of the *greatest Wits* in the County, **[middle column]** to be nominated at the *Assembly* by a Majority of the *Ladies*, who would very naturally have chosen Gentlemen of the *greatest Estates*. Or, perhaps I could have rais'd the Price of myself higher, by proposing to be dispos'd of by *Auction*, and sending to *London* for some experience'd and eloquent *Auctioneer*. All these tempting Offers and Schemes I have resisted; and, thro' the Art and Fidelity of my *Confidant*, who conveys my Letters to you, my *real* Name is still a *Secret*, tho' much Industry, and not a little Cunning has been employ'd to detect me. The County has rung so much with my Fame, and I am become so general a *Toast*, the whole Posse of *Belles* are ripe for an Insurrection against my Dominion over the Hearts of the *Beaux*; and are ready to burst with the spiteful Things they would say of me if they knew me. Guess, now, what an entertaining Farce this must be to me, while I stand behind the Scenes, undiscover'd, and see several of my Acquaintance acting Parts in it. But, Sir, there is a Temptation to a Discovery of my Person that I had much ado to conquer, if I have *yet* conquer'd it. Your Worship (the last Man alive that I should have suspected) has enquir'd after me, it seems, with an Intention of making some Overtures in the Way of *Matrimony*. You have been sly and crafty in the Conduct of your Design, but I thought you had been enough acquainted with the World to know, that *Women* are more than a Match for you in the Business of *Plotting* and *Intriguing*. Indeed, 'Squire, I have been too hard for you, and have found out your *Name, Character,* and *Intention*, while *you* know no more of me than I have thought fit to tell you. I acknowledge with Gratitude the Honour you have done me, and am very sensible how advantageous a Match it would be for one of my small Fortune. If the *Reputation* of an *Husband* can reflect any Credit upon *the* Wife, or procure her any Respect from the *Publick*; if it would be any Pleasure to her to think that all the World will approve her Choice; if the Instruction of so *knowing* and *wise* a Person would be of use to her in the Direction of her Behaviour; *you* are the first Man that in Prudence I should think of. If *Precedency* be a Thing desireable (as it has been thought to be by the Generality of our Sex) the *Antiquity* of your Family, and your *Knighthood* (which will soon be conferr'd on you, for your great Services to the Publick) will entitle me to no *mean Rank*. If *Wealth* be any Recommendation, *'Squire Hooker* must have accumulated an Estate little inferior to that of a *Prime Minister*. The large *weekly* Profits of so *taking* and *popular* a Paper; the many *Presents* that are *daily* made you; the many *Legacies* (larger than that given to Mr. *Chubb* for his Tracts,[28] or Mr. G—d—n[29] **[right column]** for the *Independent Whigs*) that

---

28 Thomas Chubb (1679–1747), lay Deist, *A Collection of Tracts, on Various Subjects* (London, 1730).
29 Thomas Gordon (d. 1750). "Gordon's *Independent Whig*, published in two parts in December 1719 and January 1720, proved a success: it went through five editions in

have been and will be left you; would put me on a Level with any *Duchess* in Affluence and Grandeur. These, Sir, are confessedly very inviting Circumstances to a *Woman*; but I am sorry to tell you, if I alter my Condition, I have determin'd, absolutely, to marry one of *the Cloth*. This may seem to some an odd Kind of a Fancy, at this Time of Day; but *Great Wits*, you know, have always some *Whims*, and affect to do out-of-the-way Things to be talked of. But, really, I have more honourable Motives than this, for my Resolution. *Generosity*, I own, is rather a *Male* than a *Female* Virtue; but I happen to be of a *peculiar* Disposition, and make it a Rule with me, to encourage a *weak* Party. The *Clergy* are not, at present, in the highest Estimation with the *fashionable* World, and I have an Inclination to support their Credit by the Countenance of my Choice. Besides, I am in good earnest a *Christian*, and I think it may be of some Service, if a Lady of *Taste* and *Credit* will bestow so singular a Mark of Favour upon a *Christian Priest*. After so great a Distinction shewn the *Order*, I answer for all the *Beaux* and *Smarts* of this County, that not one of them shall dare, for the future, to pronounce the Word *Parson* with a scornful Tone, or *sneer* at the Sight of a *Black Gown*. I am in hopes of bringing several *eminent Beauties* in several Parts of the Kingdom into this Scheme. Some of us in this County have already concerted Measures for effecting it, and have written to our Correspondents in other Counties, who come heartily into it. A late *Act* of *Parliament* having hinder'd us from leaving by *Will* any Part of our Estates to the *Augmentation of Livings*,[30] we are determin'd, in our *Life time*, to settle Ourselves and Fortunes, *unalienably*, upon the *Clergy*, as the strongest Proof we can give of our *Piety*; and we humbly hope this our good Intention will not be censured as a fraudulent Evasion of the Design of the *Legislature*.[31] As we have not been very anxious to conceal a Purpose that we need not be ashamed of, it has already taken Wind, and raised the utmost Surprize and Consternation amongst the *Toupees*, the *Solitaries*, &c. A Knot of them have already put their Heads, with all their Appurtenances of Ribbands, &c. together, to contrive how to defeat so *barbarous* a Design against every Thing that is *polite, genteel,* or *rational*. They agreed (as I am informed by Mr. *Simple*, whom I keep in *Countenance*, as *Ministers of State* keep Spies in *Pay*, for such Kind of Uses) to

---

one year, and was translated into French, and in 1720 Gordon and Trenchard started a weekly paper of the same name. The powerful anti-clerical polemic of this periodical led to attempts by some of the clergy to suppress it, and Gordon's response, *The Craftsman* (1720), was again very popular, and reprinted several times in Britain and America." *ODNB*.

30 Richardson was printing the House of Commons journals and was a close friend of its distinguished Speaker, Arthur Onslow. Maslen, pp. 22–26.
31 See Introduction, footnote 3 and discussion above.

make Application to all their Friends in the *House of Commons*, that a Bill may pass next Sessions, *for the better Regulation of* MARRIAGES among *the* CLERGY, *and restraining* BEAUTIES, *or* GREAT FORTUNES **[next page]** *from throwing away themselves, to the great Grief of their Relations and Friends, and the Prejudice of the Publick:* Provided, however, that this Bill, intended only for the *Established Clergy,* be so drawn up as not to affect any *Dissenting Teacher,* of what Denomination soever. One Clause of this intended Bill provides, that no *Parson* whatsoever (below the *Bench*) shall marry a Woman worth upwards of 500 *l.* Sterling; or one who has all her Limbs, a strait Shape, a tolerable Complexion, or a regular Set of Features; they deeming it highly inexpedient, that *Clergymen,* whose *Calling* is of a *spiritual* Nature, should indulge in *fleshly* Pleasures, or in *Pomps* and *Vanities.* An Objection against this Clause was started, but soon over-rul'd. Mr. *Sprightly* said he did not see why the *Clergy* should not have *pretty Wives* as well as other People; if for no other Reason, yet for This, that such *pretty Fellows* as They might have the Satisfaction of making *Cuckolds* of the aukward Curs.[32] But this was fully answer'd by Mr. *Sly,* who observ'd That as to *Beauty* in the Business of *Adultery,* there was no great Matter in it; that *Variety* would be a sufficient Temptation to Gentlemen of *Gallantry,* and the Joke upon the *Parson* full as clever. There was a good pleasant Debate about another proposed Clause. One who had more Zeal than Discretion, was of Sir *Sampson Legend's* Opinion in the Play. Sir *Sampson,* for the Honour of his ancient House, was minded to make a *Great* Man of his eldest Son, and a *Beggar* of the youngest. The unfortunate Youth, notwithstanding he was in this poor Condition, found himself still possess'd of his *Appetites,* and desir'd something of his Father wherewith he might satisfy them. The testy old Knight broke out into the most passionate Exclamation, that such a *Scoundrel,* as he was, should presume to have *Appetites, Passions,* &c. So this Gentleman could not imagine what such pitiful, despicable *Scrubs* as *Parsons,* should do with Inclinations of so genteel and elegant a Nature as the Love of the Fair Sex; or if they were so sawcy as to pretend to Pleasures that belong to their *Betters,* they should be reprimanded and restrain'd. He, therefore, was clearly of Opinion, that a Clause should be inserted, prohibiting all Clergymen the Comforts of *Matrimony.* His Neighbour, who was a great *Patriot,* said, *That* was downright *Popery,* and would bring in the *Pretender.* Another took Notice, That in spite of all their Pains, in endeavouring to root out *Superstition,* many of the *weaker* Sex would still have a Regard for the *Parsons,* and, taking their *seemingly* hard Case into Consideration, might be induc'd to have a little *Pity*

---

32 "1.b. 1600 *figurative.* As a term of contempt: a surly, ill-bred, low, or cowardly fellow." *OED.*

on them; and, therefore, that such a Prohibition might be attended with some Inconveniences to themselves. But Mr. *Blunt* put an End to the Debate, with a short but pithy Speech: 'As to the *Protestant Interest*, it is safe enough. Let the *Clergy*, by *Celibacy*, be ever so much *detach'd* from the common Interest of the Nation, if they have neither *Money* nor *Power*, they can do neither Hurt nor Good. As to our *Wives* and *Daughters* they can be in no great Danger from them, while we take Care to make them so *odious* and *contemptible*. But *here* lies the great Point of all: We must make them all as *poor* as we can, that they may be *inconsiderable*, and therefore let the **[middle column]** Rogues *marry* and *get Children* as fast as they will; this must make them still *poorer*, and answer our Intention better than the *Quakers Bill*."[33]

It appearing from this and other Instances, that the Reputation of the *Clergy* is very low amongst our Polite People, it is high Time for some generous Spirits of Credit and Interest to support them. For this Reason, Sir, is you have any Thoughts of making a Tender of your Worship's Person to *Belinda*, you must forthwith repair to the *Bishop*, and enter into *Orders*. I would not have you, out of *Affection*, devote yourself to so *sacred* a Profession, without a *proper Call*. But a Person of your Sentiments and Dispositions cannot be without a suitable Inclination to the Office; as a Person of your Wisdom cannot want a sufficient Motive in Respect to *worldly Interest*; it must make your Fortune: Consider how much Pains you have taken, how much Zeal you have shewn in the Service of *Christianity*, the *Hierarchy*, and the *Church of England*, and what a natural Recommendation this will be to the Favour of the *whole Order*. A fat *Rector*, and an *Arch Deacon* you will be upon the very first Vacancies; not so much out of regard to your *personal* Merit (which I allow to be *very great*) but in Honour of the Cause in which you are engag'd. Can you imagine that while all other *Weekly Journalists* ride in their Chariots, and are distinguish'd by their *Party*, that the only *Weekly Advocate* for *Religion* should be unrewarded? But, however, for Fear you should not be *Knighted* before you are *Ordained*, and should be forc'd to wait some Time for a *Bishoprick*, I must insist upon it, as a Preliminary Article in the *Treaty*, that you immediately take your *Doctor's Degree*. Not that I trouble myself about *Place*, but only for the Sake of humbling 'Squire *Lofty*'s Wife, who values herself mightily upon her Husband's living in the same House where his Ancestors, for 500 Years, have *Eat, Drank, Slept,* and *Walk'd* about, without being oblig'd to do any Thing else. When you have comply'd with my Condition, pray signify the same to

Belinda.

Northamptonshire.

---

33 See *The True Briton,* footnote 27. Mr. *Blunt* seems to be emulating Swift's ironic persona in *A Modest Proposal,* where children were regarded as an economic expediency.

6. *Weekly Miscellany*, No. CLXXXVI (186). Saturday, July 17, 1736

I am at present in an odd Situation; under the Displeasure of a *Young* Lady (as I imagine from the Sprightliness of her Compositions) and in relation to an Affair of so delicate a Nature that I know not how to make a proper Defence, or a proper Confession. She is pleas'd to charge me with having express'd a strong Inclination to be better acquainted with her; and not to plead guilty to *This* Accusation, would be an Impeachment of my own Taste, and a Crime that I could not forgive myself. But then, by this Acknowledgement, I bring upon myself the Imputation of *Inconstancy*, and a Character that is not very agreeable even in a *Woman*, but intolerable in a *Man*; that of a *Coquet*, for admiring the Lady so much *before* she said civil Things to me, and taking no Notice of her *afterwards*. I find the Lady's Emissaries are not always so exact in their Intelligence; for I have still continued to express, and really retain, the same Regard for her; tho', not having so much Vanity as to think she was in earnest in her Matrimonial Overture, I did not seem forward to accept it. I chose rather to give her the Opportunity, which she has taken and improv'd, to reproach me with Want of *Gallantry* in slighting her Offer, than to give her Occasion to banter me for my *Folly*, in thinking she really intended to make one. But I cannot help making an Observation on the *Female Sex*, that may be of Service to such of *ours* as are not so well acquainted with their Temper. If a Lady has a real Inclination that a Gentleman should make his Court to her, and he has not Sagacity enough to perceive it, she despises him; if he wilfully neglects to take the Hint, she never forgives him: Her Esteem turns into Scorn, and her Love into hatred. *Belinda* only wanted to be *merry*, and to be *witty*; and I heartily forgive her *Mirth* for the Sake of her *Wit*. I am much pleased with her intended Correspondence, and make no doubt but my Readers will be so too. I only wish that her Observations on such useful Subjects may fall into the Hands of more *Ladies* and *Gentlemen* of *Fashion*, than are likely to enquire after so *unfashionable* a Paper as the *Miscellany*.

R. HOOKER.

Bless me! What Flesh alive would have thought that such a sober, sedate Sort of a Creature, as 'Squire *Hooker* seems by his Writings to be, should have so much of the *Coquet* in him! While the Success of your Enquiry after me was doubtful, you was eager in the Pursuit, and had all the painful, pleasing Anxieties of a Lover; alternately cast down with Fear, and lifted **[middle column]** up with Hopes; now dejected, forlorn and dismal as the *Knight with the Sorrowful Face*, then all on Fire with Expectation, Joy dancing in your Eyes, and smiling in every Feature; in short, either *melancholy* or *raving* mad. *Belinda* was the Object of your *waking* and *sleeping* Thoughts, the constant Subject of your Conversation; but now I have made some Advances, like other forward Girls. I am slighted by you. As I told you, I have continual Spies upon you; and I could refresh your Memory with particular Instances of your Passion; but I have too great a Contempt for the Indifferency wherewith you receiv'd my Offer, to give myself so much Trouble. By not taking any Notice of it, you have *refus'd* me; and I must take the Liberty to tell you, I think myself well off; for I doubt I should have had but a very queer kind of an Husband of you, with such a Pack of aukward Humours, and stubborn ill Habits, as *Old Batchelors* generally acquire. As you are a good, honest, well-meaning Man, who has seen something of the World, you may be well enough qualified to read wholesome Lectures of *Morality* to the young Ladies, and teach them their Duty; but my *Aunt* and her *Chaplain*, I thank them, have taken such Care of my Education, given me such Plenty of good Instructions, and put me into so good a Way of improving myself farther, that I have no Occasion for a *Tutor*. I am for no Lectures, unless they be *Curtain Lectures*,[34] and, as I have been told, it is none of the *Husband's* Business to read them: So, Good 'Squire, your most humble Servant. You may look as miserable, be as much out of Humour as you please, if your *Breakfast, Dinner,* and *Supper* are not ready to a Minute: You may be as peevish and fretful as you please, if any Body offers to put you out of your Way; you may go to Bed at your own Time; you may wear as many Night-Caps as you think necessary; get another Flannel Waistcoat, if your Constitution requires it: You may get a Pair of Spectacles, a Spitting Pot, or any other such Indications of Wisdom and Experience; and if you can meet with any Body that will take a Liking to such venerable Matters, the Lady shall be welcome to take them all, and your Worship into the Bargain: I promise you I do not intend to forbid the Bans. As to keeping up a civil Correspondence with you, I have no manner of Objection against it. For, amongst many other ridiculous and absurd Customs, I have always thought it one, that if there has been a Courtship between a Gentleman and a Lady, and it goes off, they must take their final Leave of one another, and never see each other after: That is, because they are well acquainted, and like one another's Company, therefore they must break Friendship. Indeed, if I were so desperately **[right column]** in Love with your Worship, that writing to you might be the Means of keeping up a Fire in my Breast, that would endanger my Life, or consume my Peace and Quiet, it would be highly improper to deal in any such inflammatory Things, as *Pen, Ink,* and *Paper*. But since it is my good Fortune not to be in Danger of dying such an unnatural Death, or of living so miserable a Life, I shall be glad to keep up my Acquaintance with you; and

---

34 'A reproof given by a wife to her husband in bed' (Johnson)." *OED*.

the rather, because it is possible, that some other People may be the better for it. But methinks I see a venerable Person most violently discompos'd, and hear him express a Mixture of Grief and Indignation, that the *Dignity* of the *Miscellany* should be debas'd by the low Prattle of an idle Girl. Poh—says *old Gruff*, and down goes poor *Belinda* upon the Table. Nonsense! Stuff! *Love in the Miscellany* is as bad as *Love in a Hollow Tree*.*35 A third only reads my Name, and serves my Letter as many other *Love-Letters* have been served, returns it— Here—*Tom*—run after the Woman, give her the Paper again, and bid her bring no more of them. Then slap goes the Door, and the House shakes; the good Man takes a hasty Turn or two about the room to give some Vent, then walks awhile in the Garden to cool himself, then calls for a Bason of Water to *purify* his Fingers from the contracted Pollution, then reads a Chapter in *Job*, and grows pretty patient and quiet. But after all, Mr. *Hooker,* what is this great Disturbance about? Have I talk'd *Blasphemy* or *Obscenity?* If these honest Gentlemen do not like *Love-Letters*, they need not read them. When we go to *Church*, we are obliged to hear *them out*, whether we like what they say, or not; but it is not so bad with *them* in this Case: If they dislike a Subject, or the manner of treating it, they may pass it over, and hope for a better next Week. If we gay, young Folks were as captious, you give us Occasions enough to quarrel with you. But your Paper is a *Miscellany*, and your Readers are *Miscellaneous*. If they would keep their Temper, and wait the Issue, perhaps they may find my Correspondence less trifling and insignificant than they expect. I have the same grave Design with the gravest of your Readers; and if I carry it on with more Chearfulness and Humour, the Instruction will be more pleasing, and the Success not less. The *Ladies*, next to the *Clergy*, (and I question whether I need except *them*) have it more in their Power than any other Persons in the Kingdom, to reform the *Principles* and *Manners* of the *Gentlemen*; and if I can do any Thing towards uniting the Interest of our Sex in the Service of *Religion* and **[next page]** *Virtue*; your Readers ought to give me Leave to do it in my own Way. If I were in the *Pulpit*, I would endeavour talk in a Manner becoming the Place; but in a *Weekly Paper*, a *little Pleasantry*, if one happens to have Spirits enough, or a *little Wit*, if one can afford it, may not be unseasonable or unacceptable. If it were not for the Vanity of the Application, I would quote an Answer of an ingenious Author to another, who complain'd of him for being Jocular and Satyrical: He thought it hard that he should be condemn'd *for being what Nature made him; it might have pleased God to have made his Adversary a*

---

35 "*A Comedy written by a Grave Lord.*" William Grimston, Viscount (1683?–1756), *The Lawyer's Fortune, or, Love in a Hollow Tree: A Comedy* (1705). Aaron Hill was probably the source of this reference to the contemporary theater.

Wit too. As I intend to form an *Association* of *Beauties* against *Infidelity* and *Immorality*, I hope to contribute something towards making them still more beautiful and giving them the greater Influence. If I can help to improve their Understandings, correct their Notions as to *Love* and *Marriage*, teach them how to behave to their *Humble Servants*, and give them proper Rules for the Regulation of their Choice of *Husbands*, I shall be the Means of doing good Service; the Advancement of *Religion* and *Virtue* depending greatly on the Sentiments and Conduct of the Sex, in these important Points. Lord *Halifax*, in his *Advice to his Daughter*,[36] has given very sensible Directions for the Behaviour of a *Wife*, according to the particular Temper of the *Husband*; but it is very strange that he should give her no Rules for making a proper *Choice* of one; since it is much easier to *prevent* an Evil, than to *cure* it. To bear Misfortunes with Patience is a *Virtue*; but to endeavour to avoid them is but *common Prudence*. But the Conduct of a Lady *before Matrimony*, especially in That nice and delicate Affair of *Courtship*, requires the greatest Share of *Wisdom* and *Honour*, at an Age when she has had little Experience, and is supposed to have less Thought and Reflection. What the *Virgin* and the *Mistress* is, such will probably be the *Wife*. If a Lady behaves improperly to a *Lover*, it is not likely that she should behave well to her *Husband*. If she carries *no* Sentiments, or *wrong* ones, with her into the State of Matrimony, she seldom makes much Improvement afterwards: But if in her *Single* State she began to exercise and improve her Understanding, if she accustom'd herself then to Caution and Circumspection in her Behaviour; she will most probably afterwards go on to make greater Improvements; because one principal Part of her Prudence will be to chuse an Husband who is a Person of Discretion and Virtue, who may be helpful to her both by *Instruction* and *Example*, in the Enlargement of her Knowledge, the Direction of her Conduct, and the perfecting every Religious and Virtuous Disposition. In the Course of these Subjects there will be frequent Opportunities, and, as the World goes, there is great Occasion, to make some Observations concerning the Conduct of *Parents*, who ruin vast Numbers by their *Neglect*, or *Indiscretion;* or offer them up a Sacrifice to their own *Pride* and *Vanity*, *Avarice* and *Ambition*.

But it will be asked, How I can pretend to be qualified to write on such difficult Subjects as these? I do not pretend to it. For my *Materials* I am beholden chiefly to my *Aunt's* and the *Chaplain's* MSS, which are all in my Possession, and left me (to tell **[middle column]** you the Truth, Mr. *Hooker*) with a

---

36 *The Lady's New Year's Gift* (1688) by George Savile, Marquess of Halifax (1633–1695), was popular advice book on what to do if married to a drunkard, on how to arrange one's domestic affairs, on raising children, etc.

Command that I should digest them as well as I could under proper Heads, and publish them in the *Miscellany*. My *Aunt* was a Person of a most excellent Understanding, and Acuteness. In her *Youth* (which was at the latter End of the gay and witty Reign of *Charles* the Second)[37] having a good deal of Life in her Constitution, a good Fortune, and a great many fashionable Relations and Acquaintance, *she* kept great Variety of genteel Company, and had uncommon Opportunities of seeing and remarking the Errors and Vices of the World, tho' thro' the Care of her Parents, and her own good Sense, she had Virtue and Prudence enough to avoid them. To the very last she preserv'd the Cheerfulness of her Temper, and a quick Relish for Conversation; but was more nice in the Choice of her Companions, spent less Time in Company, and the common Amusements of Life, that she might have the more for her Favourite Pleasure, *Reading* and *Writing*.

The *Chaplain* (who died a little after my Aunt) was a Person of a clear Apprehension, sound Judgment, and well read in the common Branches of his Profession; but his particular Excellency seem'd to lie in a happy Way of making *Moral Reflections*, and stating accurately the *Relative* Duties; so that his Papers will supply me where I stand most in need of Assistance, in settling the Bounds of *Paternal Authority*, and the Extent of *Filial Duty*, in respect to *Matrimony*;[38] and shewing from the Consideration of *Human Nature* and *Human Life*, whence the greatest Degree of *Rational Happiness* must arise.

As to my own Ability, it signifies nothing how small it is; for I give you Liberty to correct or improve any Thing that comes from

BELINDA.

7. *Weekly Miscellany*, No. CXCVIII (198). Saturday, October 9, 1736

To Mr. Hooker.

SIR,

If you remember, I told You, I had several MSS. of my *Aunt's*, which I would communicate to You as Occasion should offer, and Conveniency serve. The

---

37 Charles II (1630–1685), King of England, Scotland, and Ireland from the 1660 Restoration of the monarchy until his death in 1685.
38 In his correspondence with Sarah Chapone, Hester Chapone, Frances Grainger, and other young women, Richardson enjoyed endlessly debating the "Bounds of Paternal Authority." *Belinda*'s praise of the Chaplain here barely disguises his real identity as Richardson himself!

Inclosed had this Title to it, *The Copy of a Letter sent to my Niece—on Occasion of a Dream*. The *Chaplain* being dead, I can give no Account of the Circumstances of the Young Lady of her Father, but there is a great deal of tender Affection in the Composition, and it will suggest useful Hints of *Children* and *Parents*.

Yours,

BELINDA.

"I wish to God, my Dearest Child (for so I must esteem you) was either in Heaven, or in the Arms of some honest, good Man, who would make her happy in this World by a virtuous Affection, and by his useful and agreeable Conversation, and good Example help to secure and increase her future Felicity. I never was so sensible as now of the Significancy of the old *English* Proverb, *As busy as a Hen with one Chick*. I have one only Child; and, tho' I am but an *Adopted* Parent, I find in myself all the tender Anxiety and careful Sollicitude of a *Natural* One. My Invention is continually on the Stretch, to find out all possible Ways of making her happy, and my Imagination as busy in forming to itself the several Accidents that may happen to render her miserable. *Sleep*, that quiets all my other Cares, does not interrupt my Concern for her Welfare. Last Night I suffer'd a great deal of Pain, and enjoy'd a great deal of Pleasure, by seeing her in different States. In a *Dream* I saw my Girl, (who, must be allow'd to be very genteel, and has a much politer Taste) married to a little, whiffling Fellow, a Compound of insipid Pertness, Ignorance and Folly, because he had good Business, and could buy her fine Cloaths. What a world of disquieting Thoughts crouded in upon my Mind on this Occasion. *Now* I fansy'd her gradually sinking down to the Size of his Understanding, till his low Conversation became not only tolerable, but agreeable. *Then*, again, I view'd her inwardly discontented; asham'd of his idle Prattle and as idle Behaviour; receiving no Satisfaction in any thing that he said, or did, because she could not love him; and not able to love him, because she could not esteem him; nor esteem him for Want of rational Perfections; true to his Bed, only from a Sense of Religion, but not out of any Inclination to the Man; rather bearing his Conjugal Caresses, because it was her Duty, than receiving them as an Enjoyment: Wretched State! Unhappy Girl! How she languish'd, grew pale and sickly! How her Charms faded, her Spirits decay'd, her Temper chang'd from an innocent Spriteliness to a settled Melancholy, interrupted sometimes by short Fits of forc'd Mirth; forc'd out of good Nature and Complaisance! Methought **[next page]** one Night, when she was alone, comparing her improper Companion with the more agreeable Persons of her Acquaintance, she fetch'd a deep Sigh, at which I awoke; but soon fell asleep again thro' the Fatigue I had suffer'd by her Imaginary

Distress. Another Scene, still more afflicting to me, presented itself to my disturb'd Imagination. The Affairs of her Family were all settled, and her *own* Father in a Condition to advance an handsome Fortune in ready Money. Such a Fortune requir'd a Settlement; and deserv'd a *Gentleman* of considerable *Fashion*. Such an one, either for the Sake of enjoying a pretty Woman that he could have no Hopes of debauching, or some other indirect Motive, offer'd himself, and was accepted. For a little while, so long as Curiosity lasted, he was pleas'd with her; but the Itch after *Variety*, which is never to be satisfy'd, soon made her indifferent to him, and him cold to her. He whor'd on as he did before he marry'd, and gave her the Foul Disease.[39] He seldom was at home, but when he had his rakish Companions along with him. Bawdry, Swearing, and Jests upon Religion were her frequent Entertainment. If she went to Church, or said her Prayers, she was laugh'd at for her Weakness. By Degrees she fell insensibly into an irreligious Habit, tho' her natural Modesty preserv'd her from running into his profligate Immoralities. She liv'd without thinking of God that made her: She dy'd full of Horror and Despair, fore-tasting that Torment which she was going to endure for ever. Dreadful, shocking Thought! I started up in my Bed, but the Disorder of my Spirits, before I was well awake, threw me into a senseless Confusion, that soon clos'd my Eyes again. Oh blessed Change! From Darkness to Light! from Misery to Happiness hereafter! I *now* saw her marry'd to an *honest, virtuous* Man; who, tho' he had not better natural Parts than she, had more Sense, because he had more improv'd them, and more Judgment, because he had more Experience. He was continually studying how to improve her Understanding, and to fill her Mind with just Notions and proper Sentiments. It was surprizing, even to herself, to see what an Alteration there was in her Thoughts, her Conversation, and her Looks. A Consciousness of her acting and thinking rightly gave her a continual Satisfaction, Serenity and Joy: Her inward Content of Mind gave an Evenness to her Temper, a Chearfulness to her outward Behaviour and Appearance. She was easy to every Body, and under every Occurrence, because she was easy *within*. She grew more and more agreeable, and more and more happy. The Perfections of the Mind were daily added to those of the Body; the Graces united with her Charms, and even beautified her Beauty. She every Day grew better pleas'd with her Husband, because she every Day grew better pleased with herself, and was sensible that her *Self-Complacency* was, in a great measure, owing

---

39 "Originally: designating disorders characterized by (supposed) putrefaction, or by the production of pus or malodorous excretions. In later use: *spec.* designating infectious diseases, esp. syphilis; chiefly in **foul disease**. Now *historical.*" OED.

to his affectionate Care to improve her. He every Day grew more fond of her, because she every Day grew **[middle column]** more lovely, and more loving. They both improv'd in Happiness, as they improv'd in Virtue, and mutual Love; and they improv'd in Virtue by the mutual Influence of each other's Conversation and Example. O virtuous, happy Pair! happy in themselves, and in one another! Supporting each other under the *Evils* of Life, and doubling each other's *Joys* by Participation! To such a Pair, so confirm'd in virtuous Habits, and so united in virtuous Affection, every Incident of Life gives Pleasure. A kind Expression, or a kind Look, is to them an higher *Enjoyment* than the highest *Sensual* Pleasure of others; and *their* Sensual Pleasures, *their* Conjugal Enjoyments, greatly heighten'd by the Tenderness of their Passion; refin'd, sublimated, and, as it were, spiritualized, by partaking of the *Mind,* and not arising wholly from the *Body.* As it is impossible for *Lust* to give so much Pleasure as *Love*; so 'tis impossible for a *Vicious* Man to love a Woman so well, so much as a *Virtuous* Man can. This is a Secret to most *Ladies,* who have not consider'd the Nature of Things, but as great a Truth as any in the Bible. The Reputation which they both gain'd by their Behaviour, and the Respect paid them by the World imported Foreign Pleasure to that Stock at home which their mutual Affection afforded, because it helped to increase their Affection. The Fidelity and Carefulness of their Servants; the Affection, Dutifulness, and Hopefulness of their Children, owing chiefly to good Oeconomy in their Family, and a religious Education, still added to their Felicity, and made them a Blessing to others. And when they came to die, upon so rational and useful a Life! With what Rapture did they look forward into the World of Spirits, where they hop'd to meet, tho' not as *Man* and *Wife,* yet as more perfect and glorify'd Beings, more united in *Angelical* Affection, and exalted to much higher Felicity than *Flesh* and *Blood* can give us! Methought her Husband dy'd first, and the tender Solemnity of their Parting extorted a loud Shriek from her, which put an End to my Dream. May this last Fiction of my Imagination be verify'd in Fact, and prevent either of the former from becoming true of my dear Child. Tho' these are *Dreams,* they are Dreams of what *has* happen'd, and *will always* happen under the like Circumstances. If you *marry* according to either of those Descriptions, you'll find the *Consequences* no *Dream.*"[40]

---

40 This dream narrative reads like a notebook for a novelist bent on writing about the various scenarios of courtship and marriage.

8. *Weekly Miscellany*, No. CCXLIII (243). Friday, August 19, 1737

[Webster's invitation to Chapone]

As I have formerly taken the Liberty of writing to *myself* under the Character of a *Lady*, and done Discredit to the Sex by personating one of them so awkwardly, it is incumbent upon me to make what Satisfaction I can by assuring the Public of the Genuineness of the following Letter; tho' to Persons of Discernment there are such evident Tokens of the *Sex* in the *Composition* as will leave them in no doubt.[41] A peculiar Softness and Tenderness of Sentiment and an easy Sprightliness temper'd with Modesty, so distinguishable in the Writings of the *Ladies,* appear in the highest Degree in this Letter. But, as I am obliged, for the sake of explaining some Parts of *her's* to publish one of *my own* that occasioned it, I shall fully satisfy every Reader that I not only did *not* write it, but that I was no more *capable* of writing it, than of changing *my Sex*; as able to assume her *Nature* as her *Turn of Thought and Expression*. However, least Envy or Ill-nature should still raise Doubts, I must inform the Reader that I have shewn the MS. under her own hand writing, to several of her particular Friends who know it.[42]

I must detain the Reader a little longer while I give *him* some Account of the Correspondence, and the *Lady* some Account of the Publication of her Letter.

Curiosity lead [*sic*] me to read, and a great deal of strong Sense and Wit obliged me to admire, a Pamphlet, lately published by Mr *Roberts*, under the Title of, *The Hardships of the English Laws in Relation to Wives*. Expressing my high Opinion of the Performance and the Abilities of it's Author, it provoked a particular Friend of her's, and mine to tell me that it was a *Lady,* and that he had the Happiness of being intimately acquainted with her.[43] Upon this I desired him to convey to her two *printed Letters* in the *Miscellany* upon her Book,[44] with an Intimation that I intended to write her the Letter here published, and had the Pleasure of receiving her Answer by the next return of the Post. I immediately applied for Leave to *publish* it, but found

---

41 Webster's invitation to Sarah Chapone.
42 If Webster has no idea of the author's identity, as he later asserts, then how does he know "several of her particular Friends" to verify her handwriting? Richardson may have been one of her "particular Friends."
43 It is possible that this "particular Friend" was Richardson, who may have helped her get the essay printed in the first place. The same phrase "the Happiness of" occurs in the letter from *Aspasia*. See *WM*, No. 132 (June 28, 1735).
44 *WM*, No. 133 (June 28, 1735); and No. 300 (October 23, 1736).

it difficult to get the better of the Lady's *Modesty,* tho' I endeavoured to gain over many of her other Virtues to my Interest. However, as I had no *express Denial,* our Friend, who undertook absolutely for her Consent, has now undertaken to procure her Pardon for publishing without any *formal Leave.*[45] If I have given the Lady any Pain by offering this Violence to her Inclination, I hope I shall give her an equivalent Satisfaction by the Credit she will gain, the Pleasure she will communicate to a great many, and the Good she may do by her future Correspondence. As unwilling as she was at first to appear in a public Paper, she may by degrees grow reconciled to the Thoughts of it, and by habit lose that criminal Modesty which would hinder her from being more agreeable and useful by becoming more known."[46]

To the Lady who wrote the Hardships of the *English* Laws in Relation to Wives.

Madam,

I sent you two Letters publish'd in the *Weekly Miscellany* upon your Ingenious Book relating to *The Hardships of the* English *Laws*

[middle column]

concerning Wives [sic],[47] and now I take the Liberty of writing to you myself; tho' I know no more to *whom* I am writing than you know my real Name, Character, or Circumstances. Our Correspondence is something like a Conversation in *Masquerade,* but enter'd into with more innocent Intentions, and carried on with more Modesty than those Nocturnal Dialogues are. I cannot but look upon the *Advocate* for your Sex, and *'Squire Hooker,* as two Persons so very extraordinary in our way, we ought to be better acquainted. In an Age when so little Pains is taken to improve the Understandings of the

---

45 Apparently Chapone was disturbed to have her private letter made public, and Webster asked Richardson to intercede to get her pardon for the liberty taken. Years later Richardson had a similar task of calming Elizabeth Carter's nerves after his unauthorized printing of her "Ode to Wisdom" in *Clarissa.*

46 Webster hints that maybe Chapone will eventually contribute to the *WM.* The first letter by *Delia,* No. 290 (July 14, 1738), would fit in with this assumption of her relenting in her refusal to contribute.

If we take Webster at his word here, he did not read *Hardships* before the two letters appeared in his *Miscellany* (No. 133, June 23, 1735; and No. 300, October 23, 1736). But his admiration of the pamphlet and his desire to have Chapone write more things for the *Miscellany* are unequivocal. Even more significant are his hints of Richardson's complicity in encouraging her to contribute to the journal.

47 *WM,* No. 133 (June 23, 1735); and No. 300 (October 23, 1736).

Women, and so much Pains is taken to corrupt the Morals and Principles of the Men, a Lady that is capable of writing with great Strength and Perspicuity, and a Gentleman that believes his Religion, and has Zeal enough to defend it, are very great Curiosities in their kind. But as you, Madam, have shewn what the *Fair Sex* can do, whenever they think fit to exercise the fine Talents which Nature has given them, I hope Example will have some Effect towards making the *'Squires* less ashamed of appearing in Defence of their Faith. Be that as it will, I am determin'd to *persevere*; and I dare be positive that, if you would come into my Assistance, the Undertaking will no longer be thought Romantic, nor the Execution of it below the Notice of the smartest Fellows about Town. The Design of the *Miscellany* is as extensive as *Your Genius* seems to be; and it will be almost as difficult for you to think of any Subject that will not be proper for the Paper, as to write any thing that will not be an Ornament to it: But, as more Public Matters will permit, I have an Intention to publish several Letters for the particular Service of the *Ladies*, upon very useful and new Subjects; such as the Behaviour of *single* Ladies to *Gentleman*; particularly to a Gentleman that makes his Addresses; concerning the Choice of a Husband, &c. by way of Supplement to *Lord Halifax's Advice to a Daughter*.[48] That judicious Writer has given excellent Directions, but has omitted them where they are most wanted; when your Sex are in the most *critical* Circumstances, before their Judgment comes to Maturity, or they have gain'd any Experience. Thro' the Ignorance of some Parents and the Neglect of others, many innocent Creatures come into a vicious, designing World, so utterly unacquainted with it, and so much at a loss to know how to conduct themselves in it, that, let their natural Modesty and good Sense be ever so great, they must often be guilty of Improprieties, and be drawn in to *Inconveniencies*, if not betray'd into *Vices*. And as to the most important Article of their whole Life, and what will have a great Influence on their future Welfare, I mean, the *Choice of a Husband*; Parents generally have as little considered it, and judge as ill of it, as the Children can do. The *Authority of Parents* in the Disposition of their Children in *Marriage*, and the Direction of them in their Behaviour towards their *Lovers*, has been very greatly abused, for the Gratification of a tyrannical or avaricious Temper, and to the Corruption of the most innocent Minds in their Notions of *Sincerity* and *Honour* in Matters that require an Observance of the strictest and nicest Rules.[49] These Points, Madam, will require the Acuteness of your Observations, and the Delicacy of your Pen;

---

48 See footnote 36.
49 Again, Richardson's central theme in his circle of correspondents and novels.

and you must excuse my Freedom if I tell you, that, if you refuse *Religion* and *Virtue*

[right column]

the Benefit of your uncommon Abilities when they stand so much in need of your Help, I shall suspect your Faith as much as I admire your Parts; but in better Hopes I beg Leave to subscribe myself.

Madam,
Your most Obedient,
Though unknown,
Humble Servant,
From the Temple,
R. Hooker.

April 23, 1737

* * * *

[Chapone's reply to Webster]
To Richard Hooker, *Esq;*

April the 28th, 1737.

Sir,

I had the Honour of a Letter from you last Post, together with a printed *Address to the Ladies in general.* Your Letter was written with so much good Sense, and with such an Air and Spirit of Candour and Piety, that how unworthy soever I may think myself of the Honour done me in it, I neither dare impeach the Abilities, nor Integrity of the Author, by rejecting any Part of his praise, which like the signal Blessings of GOD, upon some of my Actions, humbles me under a Sense of unmerited Favours.

This, Sir, is my Sense of the Complimental Part of your Letter, what next falls under my Consideration, is the Matter of it. The Subjects you propose to write upon are of the highest Importance to the Community in general, and may be of particular Service to our Sex. But, alas! Sir, We are so sunk in Ignorance and Folly, that I know not who will be able to extricate us out of those Mazes of Impertinence, in which your Sex have involved us! You tell us (and we are bound upon our Allegiance to believe you) That the very End of our Creation was for your *Service* and *Delight.*—That our utmost Honour consists in your Approbation,— our highest Advancement in becoming your Subjects,—and our Truest Wisdom in submitting to your *Direction.* The Law gives us no Authority to act, and Custom, the greater Tyrant of the two, prohibits our *thinking* for ourselves. We never can rise above our first Principle, nor be rated higher than our intrinsic Valuation. If therefore we were created *merely* for you, 'tis enough if we can look Prettily *before* and do as we are *Bidden* after Marriage. That our Sex have a strong Influence upon yours is founded in Nature, no Learning can evade, no Strength subdue their Power. But this improper Treatment of the Sex has render'd it so ridiculous, that a Man is ashamed to acknowledge what he feels, or to be influenced by a Creature he has made so insignificant. To what End should you write to those who were never taught to *read*? I have once found it to little Purpose, and perhaps when you write you may find it to less, for,

— *Stars beyond a certain Height,*
Give Mortals neither Heat nor Light.[50]

There is such a mutual Relation, and close Connection, between Ignorance and Pride, that while Women are educated as they are at present, they will be fond of Flattery, and consequently **[next page]** prefer him, who has the greatest Skill in it. And so long as Men over-rate their Pretentions, and fancy themselves *superior Intelligences*, or in other Words, of a more *dignified Nature*, they never will qualify us to judge for ourselves, by allowing us a Rational Education. You see, Sir, that I take the Liberty to dissent from some of your Sentiments, in your ingenious Letters printed in your *Miscellany*, for which I beg Pardon, because I have not time at present to controvert them. Want of time indeed was the Reason why I took no Notice of those Letters, otherwise I should have made some Reply to them: though they were written in a Stile I should never chuse to engage in, having neither Inclinations to, nor Talents for Ridicule. However I was well entertained by them, and acknowledge they were Polite, and that you allowed me more than I could claim, as to my Abilities, though you allowed me less, as to my Arguments, and misrepresented my Sentiments.

After all, I would not be understood to disapprove or discourage you in your laudable Undertaking. I admire and honour you for it; and wish to GOD it were in my Power to assist you in it. After having assum'd the Confidence to publish my Thoughts, it might look like Affectation to say, That I questioned my Abilities, yet really I do, Sir, especially in my present Circumstances, which lay me under an Obligation to employ my Time in my

---

50 From Jonathan Swift, *Cadenus and Vanessa* (1726).

own Family, which is a pretty large one, yet consists mostly of Children, with whom I spend six or eight Hours every Day. My Husband and I are both so apprehensive of the reigning Impiety of the Age, that we dare not trust our Children from us, and therefore educate them ourselves; I assist as far as I am capable, which, together with the necessary Affairs of the Family, engrosses all my Time. If I have any Merit, it is in cheerfully quitting my *Book* and my *Pen*, for the *Needle* and *Distaff*, and endeavouring to do my Duty in that humble State of Life in which it has pleased GOD to place me.[51] Far from assuming the Province of Direction, I am sufficiently happy if I can make my slender Abilities of any use to my Husband, to whose generous Spirit I owe the Improvements of them, and who has therefore all imaginable Right to claim their Application to his Ease and Service. Were I disengaged from these Domestic Duties and Employments, I should with Joy embrace the happy Opportunity you kindly offer me, of improving my Understanding, and assisting your generous Endeavours for the Service of Mankind. No Proposal could be more agreeable to me. As we are utter Strangers to each other, we should be free from all those personal Prejudices, which are too apt to mix themselves in all our Researches after Truth; and to darken that natural Light of the Understanding, which, as far as it goes, is a sure Guide. For we cannot impute our Mistakes to any inbred Quality in the Intellect, because then false Judgments would be natural to it, and if so we never could be assured of any Truth, except this, That we must be always in Error.

After this plain artless Relation of my Circumstances, I hope Sir, that you will acquit me of the Charge of want of *Faith*, or Zeal for my Religion and Country, if I should continue to circumscribe my Inclinations, by not suffering them to carry me beyond Domestic Duties, till my Children shall no longer want my constant Care and Instruction. Whenever I can command a little Time, it shall be laid out as you require.[52]

I pray GOD give you Success, with every solid Pleasure arising from Learning and Piety. I am, with great Acknowledgments for the Honour you have done me,
SIR,

Your most Obedient
Humble Servant.

---

51 Ironic description of her domestic predicament as exemplary Christian wife? Yet Chapone denies having any talent for ridicule!
52 This surely leaves the door open to contribute something in the future. The last thing Chapone wants to do is to appear as an ambitious woman writer forsaking her domestic duties in the process.

9. *Weekly Miscellany*, No. CCLII (252). Friday, October 21, 1737

Letter from Belinda.

You have thought fit to be very severe, of late, upon *Insincerity* and *Dishonesty*; and let me tell you, Sir, it would not have been amiss if you had first looked at home before you ventured to make so free with your Neighbours. If a Man be an *insincere* and *dishonest* Man, who really is not what he *professes* himself to be, and what he *seems* to be, I take the 'Squire abovementioned (asking his Pardon) to be as great an *Hypocrite* and a *Cheat* as ever tied up an Arm or concealed an Eye to move the Compassion of the Spectators. You set out with great Professions of *Plainness* and *Simplicity*, and I always looked upon you as an honest, well-meaning Man, and your Performances, like yourself, sound and orthodox. I have sometimes thought it was pity your Friends did not bring you up to the *Cloth*, for by the *Methodicalness* of your Compositions, it should seem as if you would have split a Text with tolerable Discretion; and the *Gravity* of your Stile would have suited the Nature of a *Sermon* to a tittle. You have some other Qualifications which make you the fitter for a Divine of *this* Age, because you have a pretty good Genius for bearing Ridicule and Satire with great Steadiness and Composure. I would not have you think, that, in opposition to this Character, I am a going to accuse you of being a *vain Wit*; tho' a Brother, 'Squire and Brother—of your Acquaintance did very gravely bring such a Charge against you, and said, moreover, that he could prove it by several Witnesses. Whether he meant to produce his Evidence out of the *Miscellany* he did not say, neither did I ask him, being fully convinced of your Innocence. There is one Instance, very notorious, of your being in your natural Disposition, or by some strange Transformation, quite different from what you have *appeared* to be by Report and Manner of your Writings. Would any Mortal breathing have taken 'Squire *Hooker* for a *Woman's Man?* I should as soon have imagined you to be a *Dancing-master*. In the first place, you are most foully belied if you are not advancing apace towards the justly disgraceful Character of an *Old Batchelor*, and every one knows they have all, been most abominably ill used by our Sex; which they are sure to revenge by making female Follies, and the State of Matrimony the Standing Subject of their Jokes. Then, let any one read over some of your Letters signed *X*, particularly a *Poem* at the end of one of them, about the *Contradicting Sex*. Hearkee 'Squire; a Word in your Ear. You have since taken a great deal of Pains to coaks us into good Humour, but those Lines will be a Millstone about your Neck, and sink you for ever in the Opinion of the Ladies. CONTRADICTING SEX! *Mercy on us, what would the Man have?* He has taken great Pains to prove your *Natural* Right of Diminion [sic] over us, and would fain look in St *Paul* to confirm it. But pray now, what *Saint* or *Sinner* either ever gave yoor [*sic*] Sex the Privilege of being always in the *Right?* And if you are ever in the *Wrong* must you never be *contradicted?* Or must we suffer **[middle column]** you to have your own Opinions and your own Ways, be they ever so absurd, 'till we can get a Warrant to carry you before a *Justice,* or till we can send for the *Parson,* and have you confuted by *Authority?* And what then would become of those poor Women who have the Misfortune to converse with such as are above *Law* and *Gospel* too? He has hinted, that we have always the *last Word,* but *your* Sex have much oftener the *first,* and would you have all the Talk to yourselves? I can assure you, these and some other Reflections of the like Nature will not soon be forgotten, or easily forgiven. As to myself, I do not mention them out of any Resentment, but to shew what an *Hypocritical* part you have acted, sometimes appearing with a forbidding Moroseness and Solemnity, and at other times with downright *ill-nature* towards us, never, 'till very lately, betraying any thing of Softness and Gentleness of Disposition, or Courtliness of Address. But all on a sudden you become, or appear, quite a *Galant Spark.* Mr. *Courtly* himself could not have out-complimented 'Squire *Hooker* when he wrote to the *wonderful* Lady. Your Enemies make the worst use they can of this *Inconsistency* in Conduct. Your Well-wishers labour hard to reconcile the different Parts of it. *Most,* I find, are of opinion that the great Change is owing to the Influence of that, or some other agreeable Lady; and it has given them so high an Opinion of the Influence of her Charms, they are as much agog to see her, as the Town at present is to see some other Curiosities which are exhibited to View, and she would have as *surprizing an Effect* upon her Followers as Mrs *Map,*[53] Mrs *Drummond,*[54] Mr *H—y,*[55] Mr *F—r,*[56] or Mr—any body that is *the Shew* in Vogue.

You may probably apprehend that I intend to take Advantage of a Confession that you sometime since made in the Gaity of your Heart, and prove under your own Hand, that you attempted to put a *Cheat* upon the World, against the Laws of your Country, Nature, and Society, when you put on *Womens Clothes,* and attempted to pass for a *Young Lady.* I remember both the Fact and your Confession; but to do you Justice, you acknowledged at the same time the Awkwardness of the Imitation, and the Impossibility of deceiving any Persons of *Discernment* by the *Habit,* when your *Conversation* and *Behaviour* were so unsuitable to our Sex; and from hence I think it ought to be inferred in your Favour,

---

53 Sarah (née Wallin) Mapp (baptized 1706–1737) was celebrated as "Crazy Sally" for performing impressive bone-setting acts, normally a male profession. *ODNB.*
54 Mary Cunliffe, Mrs. Drummond Smith (d. 1804).
55 John Henley (1692–1756), English clergyman, "Orator Henley," was a flamboyant preacher and crowd pleaser. *ODNB.*
56 Unidentified.

that you could not be supposed to do it with an *Intention* to deceive, but out of a Frolic, by way of Diversion, or out of an high Compliment, to shew, that we are *inimitable*. Though this be a *Mitigation* of your Crime, as it acquits you of any criminal Intention, yet a *Crime* it is, because there being so many People who *want* Discernment you could not help deceiving many Persons, though you might not intend to do it; and therefore you must expect the Severity of the Law, if you commit any such Imposition upon the Public again.

But, Sir, the *Insincerity* and *Dishonesty* which I shall charge upon you are of a quite different and much more heinous Nature; nothing less than *Ingratitude, Inconstancy,* and *Breach of Promise,* quite the Reverse of what you pretended to be, or what you would be thought to be. Remember what an helpless, distressed Condition you was in; under an absolute Engagement to the Public for some Essays of *Wit* and *Humour*; incapable of answering the Demand yourself, and not knowing where to hope for Relief, the *Modern* Wits not being charitably disposed, or not well inclined to your Design. Under these forlorn Circumstances how movingly did you cry for Assistance, and how often did you cry in vain? I was affected with your Distress; with good Nature sent you some seasonable Letters to save your sinking Reputation; and partly by my Intreaties persuaded, and partly by my Example provok'd, a very rich Genius to be very liberal to you.[57] At first, you was full of Acknowledgments, and I seemed to be a great Favourite with you; which had it's natural Effect upon the Generosity of my Nature, and increased my Inclination to serve you. But, like other *Beggars,* as soon as you thought you had found out a more able and agreeable Assistance, you slighted *my* Correspondence as useless, and have suppressed my Letters, though you had acknowledged the Receipt of one, and promised to *publish* it the first Opportunity. Please to *saddle,* and rummage the *Miscellaneous* Box, and you will find a MS. of mine, bearing Date some Months since, concerning the *Folly* and *Sin* of *marrying a known Libertine* or *Infidel.*[58] But, perhaps, for the sake of *filthy Lucre* you have been induced to destroy it. As great a Stir as you make about *Disinterestedness* I have a Suspicion that one or two of my Sparks have been tampering with you (for my Letter soon took Air, and gave no little Uneasiness); and, though I must do you the Justice to own, I have a good Opinion of your *Disposition,* yet *Temptation,* and the *Frailty of human Nature,* so much complained of in your last, might prevail against Inclination. I have the more reason to suspect some such thing, from several Hints that have been dropped up and down in your Paper, that look as if your *Circumstances* were not altogether so good as you could wish them to be, or as I, when I was

---

57 This "conversation in masquerade" barely disguises Richardson's role as financial sponsor as well as printer of the *WM.*
58 Familiar theme for the author of *Pamela* and *Clarissa.*

so very fond of you, apprehended them to be; and you seem'd a little out of humour with the Public for not *rewarding* you, as it has done other Journalists, for the violent Pains you have taken, for several Years, to serve it. But that to those whom it may more immediately concern. I have no *Places* in my Disposal, except a Place in my *Affections,* and that you reacted, according to the way of the World, in hopes of one that you liked better; and you have been served, as all such *fickle* People deserve to be serv'd, for I do not find that she intends to take any more notice of you, than you do of me. Come; all Malice apart: Be *honest,* and I'll be *generous.* Publish this as soon as it comes to hand, and I'll do more for you than ever body will do.To keep up your Spirits and encourage you to go on the more chearfully. I'll *Promise* you something. Indeed, it may chance to be like some other things, a little *uncertain,* and a *good while a coming,* but a *Ticket* in a *Lottery* is worth acceptance, tho' it should be some time before it be drawn, and prove a *Blank* at last. Besides, *Waiting* is no new thing to you, and it seems to agree with you as well as with most Folks. Not to keep you any longer in suspence, provided you should outlive me, which I hope you will not do, and I should not *marry,* which I hope I shall do, I intend to make you my *Heir.* I hear it is become a Fashion with you great Writers to have *Estates* **[next page]** and *Legacies* left you, and I am willing to set a good Example; and who knows but my *Will* may be as fortunate to you as my *Wit* has been, and excite some others to think of you who have more to leave you than I have, and are likely to die before me. At present I give you the Mortification to be assured that I have some inviting Offers, and am in perfect Health.

St. James's-street,
Oct. 15. 1737. BELINDA.

To save you the Confusion of being detected, I shall send you a Copy of the Letter in a little time.

10. *Weekly Miscellany*, No. CCLXV (265). Friday, January 20, 1737/8

To Richard Hooker, *Esq;*

SIR,

As you have engaged in the great and laudable Work of endeavouring to keep alive the almost dying Flame of *Piety* amongst Us, which burns with so unsteady, and glimmering a Light, one Moment breaking out in a flash of *Enthusiasm,* and the next Sinking into the Darkness of *Infidelity,* giving but too much Ground to fear the removal of our Candlestick; So I think it an Obligation on All, who are Friends to the Sacred Cause of Divine Truth; However unqualified they may be for writing themselves, yet at least to shew their Approbation of those who are; for Praise is strickly [sic] and properly a Debt to the Praise-worthy. It is upon this Principle likewise that I beg for the Sake of yourself, the Public, and One Gentle Reader in particular, that you will by all honourable Methods, secure your Interest with your two *Female* Correspondents and Mr *Nobody*; and as they have all given undeniable Proof, that the finest Writers are still on the Side of *Virtue* and *Religion*; So it is but just, they should be told, there are still among the crowd some Readers capable of admiring them, and glad of having the Occasion. But after being very serious, I believe, Mr *Hooker*, between you and me; there can be no Harm in being a little merry. It is just this Minute come into my Head, and I can't help telling it you; that I am afraid, I have been guilty of a *Solecism*, a *Blunder*, a *Bull*; or whatever learned, or vulgar name, you will to a *Mistake*, in prefixing the Appellation of *Mr* before *Nobody*: For, as it is not declared, to which half of the Human Species *Nobody* belongs, so I see no Reason why we may not claim the honour of Nobodies Works as well as Ye.

Yet, however, far be it from me, to ascertain of what Sex the nameless Being is, but as I have always been a zealous maintainer of the Dignity of my own, so I should be extreamly pleased, and proud, if I might be allowed to clap an *S* to the end of *Mr*. Pray good Mr *Hooker*, do not throw my Letter into the Fire, not rumple it up. And put it into your waste-paper Pocket, No, nor so **[right column]** much as shrug up your Shoulders, or wrinkle your Forehead, when I mention the *Dignity* of *Womankind*, for I do not mean to encourage *Usurpation* or *Rebellion*. All I pretend to is, to raise the poor Souls, a little nearer to a level with yourselves. I would not have them treated, either as *Slaves*, or *Cyphers*, but like what they really were at first designed to be, *Help-mates* for ye: As you Sir, to your great Emolument find, if not in the capacity of a *Husband*, yet undoubtedly as a *Weekly Writer*, and therefore I hope you will always have Generosity and Gratitude enough to acknowledge it; or else, may *Belinda*, alter her Will (if she has made one) and be married to morrow, may the grave Lady quite forget you, and think of nothing but her own Family, and may *Nobody*, regard you no more than most ye do an *Old Woman*.

While you continue a Sincere Friend to Truth,

I am Sir, really Yours,

SOMEBODY.[59]

---

59 Probably Chapone.

11. *Weekly Miscellany*, No. CCLXXII (272). Saturday, March 10, 1737/38

O my Word, 'Squire, I must now acknowledge you to be a Gentleman of *Honour.* Not inferior to the *Knight* of *Gallant* Memory you dare assert the Cause of injur'd *Matrons* and *Virgins* against a very numerous Body of *prodigious Wits.* Nothing can exceed your *Courage,* but your *Generosity.* To take the Field, *singly,* against such an Army of *Giants,* is equal to any thing in Story. To go upon this hazardous and difficult Enterprize without having received any *Favours* from the Sex, and, as far as I know, without expecting any other than *Thanks* from them, shews a noble Mind; but if we are worthy of the handsome Things you have publish'd in our Defence, you cannot fail of receiving as much Encouragement as is consistent with our *Modesty* to shew you. For my own Part, Sir, you have cancel'd all *private* Dis-obligations by these *common* Services, and *Gratitude* has go the better of *Resentment.* I am afraid of seeming two [sic] *forward* in my Acknowledgement, lest I should offend, as I did before, a Person of your *nice* Taste; but I must, in the Name of Thousands, take this first Opportunity to express our Sense of your Civilities, and assure you of all the Assistance I can give you. My *Sister* has written with so much Ingenuity, it may be dangerous to my own Reputation to find any fault with her Composition; and you Sir, in your Introductory Preface have been so liberal in your Concessions, it may seem *ungenerous* in *our* Sex to lay any more Blame upon *yours.* Yet, I shall hope for both your Pardons if I make a Remark upon the *Lady's Letter* which brings a fresh Charge upon the *Men*; tho' it will acquit them of some Part of *her* Accusation. The *Lady* desires you to point out the *Batchelor* who will not promise a great deal more in the time of *Courtship* than he will perform after *Marriage.* The Truth is, your Sex is bad enough in all Conscience, but, give you your due, to my Comfort I do know several of you who really make good reasonable kind of *Husbands* enough. The Lady goes on to observe, that if the *Men,* when they offer their Addresses, would tell a Woman in *so many plain Words* that he does not intend to behave himself so well to her when he is secure of her, she would probably reject him. I believe so too truly; but can my Sister with a grave Face, ask you to be such *Wiseacres*? If you were to behave in so simple a Manner, tho' we might entertain a tolerable Opinion of your *Honesty,* we should think too contemptibly of your *Understandings* to make *good Wives,* tho', perhaps, Reasons of *Conveniency* might sometimes tempt us to accept of such *impolitick* Lovers. In excuse for our *Credulity* in giving Credit to extravagant Professions of Love and large Promises of future Kindness and Civility, she pleads an innocent Passion and want of Experience which incline us to believe *unmeaning* Pretences and entertain *delusive* Hopes. We *believe,* because we ourselves are sincere; we hope for *imaginary* Pleasure because the *painted* Esteem is agreeable. This, I confess, is often the Case with young raw Girls; and where they are imposed upon by designing crafty Fellows, long hackney'd in the Wiles of **[middle column]** their own Sex, and well acquainted with the Foibles and Weaknesses of ours, such Instances of Baseness and Treachery deserve the severest Resentment that so severe a Pen as my *Sister's* can express. These *cool Hypocrites* have so often *acted* the Lover, they can readily assume the Looks, the Voice, the Language, the Tenderness, the Rapture of Love; and all *seems* so like what the enamour'd Lady feels within, the Counterfeit is not discerned till *Matrimony* takes off the Disguise: But then *Justice* (for I'll not allow you a grain more) obliges me to own, what my *Sister* has omitted; that *young* and *eager* Lovers as often deceive *themselves,* as they do their *Mistresses*; not as to their *present* Passion and Intentions, but the *Continuance* and *Effects* of it. They say they want Words to express the Ardency and Softness of their Affection: and so they really do. They will always be as kind obliging *Husbands,* as they are assiduous, submissive, passionate *Courtiers*; and so they really think. They are *both* mistaken, because *neither* of them understand human Nature, and perhaps have had no Opportunities of doing it. Indeed, I cannot acquit them of *Imprudence* and *Insincerity* in *deifying* their Mistresses, and giving them *Perfections* which *cannot* belong to us. It does not require much Experience or Thought for a *Lover,* let his Love be ever so extravagant, to convince himself that his *Mistress* is not a *Goddess,* or an *Angel,* but a *Woman.* Nay, he certainly believes her all the while to *be* one, or else he would hardly think her a proper Object of his Affection, or a fit Person to be his Wife: And yet, these Flights, occasion'd only by the fervour of his Passion, and intended to make himself agreeable to the Object of it, help to give her an undue Opinion of her own Merit, and put her upon making exorbitant Demands of a suitable Deportment from *him*, which must terminate in Disappointment and Uneasiness. 'Tis a great and sudden Change, indeed, to be tumbled down in a few Days from amongst the *Stars* into the *Kitchen,* or the *Nursery*; and from a *Celestial Luminary,* all over *Brightness* and *Excellence,* admir'd, ador'd, to become a *Slave,* or at best an *upper Servant.* What an awkard [*sic*] Figure must the poor Creature make, just drop'd from *above* into her *sublunary* Station? But with my *Sister's* Leave, are not *we* as much to blame in *accepting* of such improper Compliments, as you are in *making* them? Yes, and more. The Pleasure of expressing their Passions and their Complaisance, both natural to all *sincere* Lovers, will sometimes make us of too strong Terms, but there must be a pretty large share of *Vanity* in *us,* if we take every thing as strictly due to us, which the extravagant Bounty of Love makes us a genteel Compliment of. I allow it would be better, if the Affair of *Courtship* could, by mutual Consent of both Sexes, be carried on in a more sober and moderate Way; if the *Lover* could satisfy his Passion with an honest and affectionate Declaration, "That his Mistress is extreamly agreeable to him, that he should esteem himself very happy if he could obtain her Affection and Consent, and that he would always endeavour to behave to her with sincere Kindness and good Manners;" such a reasonable Profession as this, if the *Lady* would be *contented* **[right column]** with it, would prevent false Hopes, extravagant Expectations, certain Disappointments, and as certain Resentments which often hinder the *Fondness* of the *Courtier* from *Settling*, after a *gradual* Change, into a *temperate and lasting Love*, as my *Sister* very well has it.

To be very serious on a very important Affair. The greatest Reproach to the Conduct of our Sex is, that we are not careful enough in that Point, which *only* can secure us from ill Treatment, and sometimes we act without any Regard at all to it. There *can* be no Safety but in choosing a *good* Man. This will not *always* do, since a Person of *real Piety* and *Virtue*, from an *innate Peevishness* or *Churlishness* of Temper, may be very troublesome, especially, where *Ill Nature* is armed with *Authority*; but the best *natural Disposition* may change with an Alteration of *Circumstances*, or *Constitution*, and the honestest *natural Notions* will be corrupted by *Vice*; and how many are there of our Sex, who not only do not object against a *Libertine* and a *Rake*, but seem to favour that sort of Character as the most agreeable, and the most likely to prove *good Husbands*; thereby betraying their want of *Judgment*, or *Experience*, and shewing too little regard to *Religion* and *Virtue*. The former can be considered only as a *Misfortune*, but the latter must be imputed to them as a *Crime*. If they do not know the *World*, they may easily know their *Catechism*. If they have not read *Mankind*, it is their own Fault if they have not read their *Bible;* which would have taught them better Rules. Besides, what can your Sex think of us? Or what reason have they to *confide* in us? Is not it natural for you to reason after this Manner? If the Lady had any *real* Virtue and Modesty she would certainly shew her *dislike* of Vice and Debauchery in the *Men*; unless she can imagine that Virtue and Modesty were Duties in the *Female* Part of the Species only. And if she thought it no Crime for a *Gentleman* to live at large *before* Matrimony, he has no reasonable Security that the *Lady* shall not think it as justifiable to please herself better, if she can, *after* Marriage. You see, Sir, I am as free to make just Concessions as you were. But now I shall be no less free in laying the *Great* load of *Guilt* and *Folly* where it ought to be plac'd. My *Sister* tenderly call'd it, *the mistaken Kindness of Relations who think it an Advantage to us to be settled*; and if we be but *settled*, no matter whether we be *happy*, or not. *Mistaken Kindness?* It may be so in *very profligate or weak* Parents, who have lost the relish of Virtue, and have no just Notions of human Life and human Happiness, and the true Source of it; but it oftener proceeds, as far as I have been able to observe, from *Pride* and *Vanity,* than from any Regard to their Children's Felicity. They consider more the *Credit* which a Match will do their Family by the Figure the Husband will make in the Neighbourhood, than any *Suitableness* of *Character, Principles, Temper, Person* and *Manner,* to make their Daughter truly happy. But I grow a little more solemn than I intended to be at present; and shall anticipate my Design of sending you some Lectures upon the Subject, collected partly from the *MSS.* of my *Aunt,* who, as I told you, was a Woman of **[next page]** excellent Parts and a perfect Knowledge of the World; and of the *Chaplain,* a Gentleman of sound Judgment and much Thought. And give me leave to say, if I can reform Parents, or rectify the mistaken Notions of young People, I shall do no little Service to my *Sex, Society* and *Religion.*

BELINDA.[60]

12. **Weekly Miscellany, No. CCLXXXIV (284). Friday, June 2, 1738**

Letter from Somebody to Nobody.

Alas! poor Nobody! I can hardly express the Concern I have been in for your very great, yet groundless Fright. Sure no Man, Woman, nor Child, was ever so afraid of their own Shadow by Moon-light, as you have been of the Phantom of your own creating; which must be less than nothing, since Nobody cannot give being even to a Shadow. Will you who declare your self of no Character, nor Sex, assume the Vanity and Self-conceitedness of the Haughtiest? And because a civil Thing has been said to you, presently put your self upon your Guard, for fear of being run away with? Good now be easy as to that, for I could give you such Demonstration of your Safety, in this particular, as would be sufficient to change your Fears into Spleen and Envy. But I forbear; and avow that I was fond enough to make you a greater Compliment than I do to every Body; nor will I recall it, because I still

---

60 While writing her defense of her sister's views on courtship and marriage, Belinda acknowledges here the redundancy of her own statement. Richardson seems to be cognizant of Chapone's stronger claim as feminist. In his own words she is the "Championess"!

think there was something of Justice in it, as it must be allowed that Nobody has its Share of Merit; the Merit of Wit and Humour: But I believe I shall not be thought to wrong the Trifle, if I say it is a little deficient in Good-Manners, and Gratitude. But what reasonable Being can expect That from Nobody, that is so very rarely to be met with from any Body? However, my Candour and Generosity, will be the greater, the less I find from others. Take Care of your self, for I am just upon the Point of making you another Compliment; which is, that I am vastly delighted with the Task of Work you have set us, and am only vexed that you have forestalled me in some of the Patterns. But since it is so, I intend to change my Design, for I hate to work by any Body's Drawings but my own; and as all the gay Colours will be employed in decking out your *Cupids*, and other fine Folks, I am resolved to work in the darkest. A sort of a dusky Yellow, that comes nearest to the Colour of a new Cord, is what I shall chiefly use. I have a double Reason for giving you the Draught beforehand; first, as it will anticipate the Pleasure of performing it, and next **[middle column]** as it will serve to remove another unjust Suspicion that you had entertained, as if I had a Mind to dissolve that Union between the Sexes that Nature and Providence has establish'd. No, I sincerely assure you, my Intention reached no farther than to aim at bringing both Sides to make better Husbands, and better Wives, than they seem at present inclined to do. Hypocrisy is so far from my Nature, that it is a painful Violence to me to act out of Character, for which Reason I cannot help saying still, that if Men are disappointed in their Hopes of Happiness when they marry, it is in a great Measure owing to themselves. While we are single they treat us like Baubles and Play-things, but the Moment we are married they expect all that is serious, prudent, and good from us. But while the Men, as Lords of the Creation, indulge themselves in all their vicious Pleasure, as if they were unaccountable to any other Lord, and regard us as insignificant Creatures, only subservient to their Interest, or Amusement, what can they expect from us but the very Behaviour they generally find? For who, even among them, would take Pains to become wise, if they were assured beforehand that (notwithstanding all their Endeavours and even Attainments) they should always be treated like Fools? Now where would be the Harm if they should allow us to be of the same Species, and consequently Rational at least, though in a lower Degree? Can there be one Instance brought of a Lion and Lioness contending who has the most Courage, or Magnanimity, or any other of those noble Qualities, we usually ascribe to them? Or a He and a She Bear, going together by the Ears, about who can climb a Tree the best? In the Name of Fortune let them that have the longest and the strongest Claws go first, who will dispute it with them?⁶¹ For my part, all I desire is, to know from whence that strange Prejudice should grow that must oblige us, right, or wrong, to believe that all Men are wise, merely because they are Men; and all Women silly, only because they are Women. If this was true in Fact, I could excuse the timorous *Nobody*, for being so desperately afraid of Petticoats; for as modest and humble, as the odd thing seems, I believe it would not quietly bear to be reckon'd a Fool, without having given some Occasion; for I doubt, that both No-bodies, and Any-bodies, are depraved enough to be more provoked at the Imputation of Folly, than of Vice it self. As to the Point of Subjection and Duty, it is quite another thing; and ought indeed to be treated of in quite another Manner. Therefore I shall leave that to my Betters, with this single Reflection, that I believe there is no Person, however narrow the compass of their Observations may have been, but has at some time, or other, seen a Son wiser than his Father, &c. &c. &c. though this does not in the least vacate the Laws of God, or Man. But this is a wide Field, and if I wander farther, I shall forget the Business that is on all hands allowed to belong to our Sex, which is working of Carpets and Hangings. Now the Pattern I design to draw, being to take in a great number of Figures, I shall lay the Scene of it in the broad part of *Paddington Road*; where round that celebrated Place,⁶² so well known to all publick Offenders, the Company shall be disposed in their proper Order: Hither I shall summons, without a Jury, or any Authority **[right column]** but that of my Pencil, all the unmarried Men, in this County (those of others, must repair to their own Places, for there will not be room for them here) that are turned of one and thirty; on each of which I shall bestow one of those becoming

---

61 "Is he not a sad wicked Man for this? —To be sure I blush while I write it. But I trust, that that God, who has deliver'd me from the Paw of the Lion and the Bear, that is, his and Mrs. *Jewkes's* Violences, will also deliver me from this *Philistine*, myself, that I may not *defy the Commands of the Living God!*" Pamela, 6th ed. (1742), Vol. I, p. 350.
62 Alludes to Tyburn, location of public hangings in this period. "Although executions took place elsewhere (notably on Tower Hill, generally related to treason by gentlemen), the Roman road junction at Tyburn became associated with the place of criminal execution for the City of London and Middlesex after most were moved here from Smithfield in the 1400s. In the 12th century, the Sheriff of London had been given the jurisdiction in Middlesex, as well as in the City of London. Prisoners were taken in public procession from Newgate Prison in the City, via St Giles in the Fields and Oxford Street (then known as Tyburn Road). From the late 18th century, when public executions were no longer carried out at Tyburn, they occurred at Newgate Prison itself and at Horsemonger Lane Gaol in Southwark." *Wikipedia*.

Salutaires,[63] mentioned above; the rest of their Habit shall, as near as I can work it, be such as they used to wear, the better to distinguish their Characters. Out of the Crowd (and I am sure I shall have choice enough) I intend to select some of the most remarkable Figures to fill the fore-ground of the Peice [*sic*]. On one Side you shall see a tall, well dress'd Fellow, looking, with the utmost Anger and Resentment, upon a Woman of a great Fortune, whom in his way of Thinking he accuses as the Cause of his Death, because she had the Sense to refuse his Addresses, that were supported by nothing but the common Talent of a good Assurance, without the Aid of either Estate, Birth, or Merit; while near this Lady, you may see half a dozen Milliners, and Mantua-makers, his equals, who by their distracted Coutenances [*sic*] shew that they would gladly have worked their Fingers to the Bone all Day and have watched half the Hours in the Night for the coming home of so fine a Husband. On the opposite Side, I shall place a Man of Fortune, who, with an Air mixed with Remorse and Tenderness, fixes his Eyes on the Face of a beautiful young Woman, whom he loved enough to have married, if she had had one Charm more, *viz.* Ten thousand Pounds; but not caring to abate of his own Price, he would have robbed her of her Innocence and her Vertue, if she would have betrayed herself, and complied with the villainous Design; which she happily escaping, he now makes dismal humble Signs to her that she would beg him of the Court, and get a parson to marry them immediately, though it were under the Gallows. Between these and nearest to the Post of Honour, I shall draw two other Figures, who shall have all the Appearances of Men of large Fortunes; the one seems, with a malicious Grin, to imitate a Smile at the pleasing Thought that he has had Interest, and Cunning enough to secure his fine Estate to the Children of his Favourite Mistress, though perhaps the right Heir (and probably the next of Kin to him too) is pining in a Prison for want of a Tenth part of it. The other, with Eyes averted, turns from a Groupe [*sic*] of Children, of different Features and Complexions, that are placed near him, accompanied by their respective Mothers, who have already shared so largely in his Estate, that there is nothing now left of it, except it be the Rent Role.[64] The Miens and Lineaments of these Women shall be worked up to such Perfection, that every Eye shall know whether they were taken out of a

---

63 "**I.2.a.1447–** The action of bringing someone or something back *to* (also *from*) a particular state, condition, belief, etc. Formerly also without construction, in positive sense: †restoration, redemption (*obsolete*). Now *rare*." *OED*.

64 "rent roll, n. A roll or register of rents; a list of lands and buildings owned by a person, together with the rents due from them." *OED*.

Kitchin or a Lady's Dressing Room; from behind a Counter, or from behind the Scenes; from the House of an honest Country Tenant, or that of an unfortunate *London* Tradesman. The rest of the Multitude must be crowded into Groupes, with profile Faces, and half heads, to fill up the Corners and other Vacancies: For as I believe this Peice [*sic*] will be full big enough to hang one side of the largest Room in *England*, so I intend to reserve all the Men, who after they are married, make faithless Husbands and careless Fathers, furnish out the other. These I do assure you shall be drawn in more melancholy Postures than any of **[next page]** the former. But I hasten to tell you, I am extremely pleased with your Preliminary articles; and were I a Party concerned, would be one of the first, that should sign them; but as I am out of the Question, I shall leave you the whole Honour of making the Peace: And therefore I do hereby nominate and appoint you Nobody, neither Knight, Squire, Matron, or Damsel, sole Plenipotentiary for this Treaty: And as I design this for my finishing Stroke, I am resolved to make your Powers as ample, and authentick as I can; and therefore put my right Name to them, which is *Joan Pope*. Now if you or any Body else are inclined to be so deadly witty as to call me Pope *Joan*, it shall be the same to me; for by whatever Name I am called, I shall assuredly be,

Some-Body.

13. *Weekly Miscellany*, No. CCXC (290). Friday, July 14, 1738

I HAVE lately been reflecting upon the secret Pleasure, that the Writers behind the Curtain enjoy, in comparison of one who writes as it were in the publick View and besides the Pleasure, I observe, there is a real Advantage in it; as it secures the Publisher, from any Imputation of Prejudice or Partiality, and his Correspondent from that of Vanity or Envy. This Reflection, as will appear, was occasioned by a very solemn, as well as pompous piece of Complaisance, paid to two Ladies, in your *Miscellany* of *June* the ninth.[65]

---

65 *WM*, No. 285 (June 9, 1738): *Hooker*'s note:
 "I could have made this Collection still more agreeable and entertaining, by adding to it some Letters from two Ladies, of whom I know no more than that any Man of Sense and Virtue would be proud to be acquainted with them, I have a strong Inclination to pay them all the Distinction which their unusual Talents and Accomplishments and their as unusual Religious and Virtuous Dispositions demand; and I had once determined to give them a Plate in this Volume, (tho' out of the Order of Time) as I have done to some others; but, upon Reflection, Self-Interest determined me to postpone

Now, if my Criticism does not fail me, in my Observations on reading your Paper, I have discovered more than two, or three, that have corresponded with Mr. *Hooker* under the Name and Character of Women; but as to the reality of the Characters, or Numbers, I do not pretend to determine, that being a Point best known to himself. As I shall very readily allow you to have an undoubted Right of bestowing your Springs of laurel on whom you please, so I must take the Liberty to say; that as an old Reader and new Correspondent, I hold, by the same Tenure, a Right to enquire on whom they are bestowed. Not that I in the least distrust either your Judgment, or your Equity; for you so far resemble the Picture of Justice, that giving Sentence with your Eyes hoodwinked, you can neither be influenced, by the Young, or Fair, nor prejudiced against the Old or Ugly. This Hood-winking puts me in Mind of the famous and diverting Play of Blind-man's Buff; a Play that I have not yet forgot, though I fairly own I am pretty far removed from Childhood; so far that I have for some Years past, been flattering my self, with the pleasing Thought that I was much wiser now, than 1 was at Twenty, But here I am sorry to see the Proverb, that says, Good Wits jump, is against me; for I find a very judicious Writer is of Opinion, that when People come to be a little in Years, they can neither express their own Meaning intelligibly, nor understand the Meaning of others rightly. But to return to Blindman's Buff. One known Rule of it is, that the blinded Person is not to be unbound though they catch another, unless they name them by their right Names. Now if you would indulge a little Female Curiosity, I would fain try at this Play, to find out, to which of your Women Correspondents (since you have reduced them to two) it is that your polite Address is directed. For, though I am no Candidate for Fame, yet I own the Ambition of desiring a Place in your Esteem; which I can no way so likely gain, as by guessing right, and falling in with your Way of Thinking; which if I do, I shall expect according to Custom to be unbound, and some other blinded in my stead; I therefore venture to pronounce in the dark, that they are the Lady once called the grave one, (for I have no other Name to call her by) and that other grave Lady who I remember writ upon a very grave Subject. The first of these is too bright an Example of domestick Vertue to be left out of a Paper, that generously and impartially celebrates deserving Women, as well as Men; and **[middle column]** the other is so much a Friend to your Cause, the

---

them. As I intend, at a proper Time, to publish another Volume, I thought it Prudent to reserve the most curious Things to quicken a decaying Appetite; and I persuade myself that those Ladies will enable me to make the Publick ample Amends for delaying so great a Pleasure, by adding their further Correspondence to the Entertainment."

Cause of Faith and Piety, that from my good Opinion of yourself, I am assured it cannot be she that is dropped. So that upon the Conclusion it must be the sprightly good-humoured *Belinda*, that errant telltroth[66] *Somebody*, and that nameless Body who writes so like her; that has, as other greater People have done, writ themselves out of Favour, by harping so long upon unseasonable and unwelcome Truths.

But as I before said, having no Claim, nor Pretension to the Bays my self, it would be perfectly indifferent to me who wore them but for one single Reason. For I am arrived at that even tranquil time of Life, that sets one above all personal Regards, or Prejudices; good Principles, good Sense, and good Humour in my Acquaintance cause my Esteem to rise, or fall, (just like the Mercury in a true well made Barometer) according as they approach to, or sink below this Standard. But this happy coolness of Temper, it is certain, very rarely accompanies Youth; so that I must again apologise for dissenting from the beforementioned Writer, in his Remarks on the Disadvantages of Age. Now this Reason of my so particularly enquiring about this Affair, may hereafter be communicated to you, if you are so obliging; as to satisfy me at present. In the mean while, I am glad to see that you are grown so fearful of coming into Scrapes; I remember a Time when you were not quite so cautious, that in fighting Blindfold you singled out a wrong Adversary, and fell foul upon a Paper, that was not at all concerned in that Quarrel; for by your own After-account it proved to be another. Then again I caught you tripping, when you forgot your self so far as to talk in a publick Weekly Paper, of a Lady's private Instructions, which makes me fear, you are no more able to keep a Secret, than the very Lady was, who so madly trusted you with one. But now if People will thus unnecessarily pull old Houses over their Heads, they have nothing else to do but to get from under them as well as they can; and all that their Friends can easily do, is to avoid bringing them into new Scapes [*sic*]. But I will go a little farther, and endeavour to help you out of one at this Time, by seriously advising you, to be more sparing of your Compliments to the Women, lest you should lose your more useful Friends the Men. It is they that in Reason, and in Honour, ought to lend a Hand to so good an Undertaking as yours; but I am afraid that the Worthy among them, will be apt to think the worse of you and your Cause, when the weak Sex are called in to your Assistance: And the Worthless, which we may suppose to be the Majority, will swear that you are entered into a Combination with the Women, to

---

66 "tell-troth, variant of tell-truth, n. A person who or thing which tells the truth; a truthful or candid person, text, etc." *OED.*

rob them, of their Prerogative of doing what they please;[67] than which you can't do a more offensive Thing. For when People think they have a Right to do any thing they will, they must needs take it ill to be told they do any thing that is wrong. You see you have already drawn down the Indignation of the worshipful Mr. *Blunt,* (for to be sure he is a Justice of Peace at least, if not a Deputy Lieutenant, by his authoritative and commanding Stile) and who knows how soon he may raise the Posse of his County, under the Pretence of **[right column]** defending their Lives and Liberties against that merciless Tyrant, *Somebody.* Whether Mr. *Blunt's* Character be feign'd, or real, is all one to me, if it be the first, (as by some particular Marks I take it to be) I look upon it as a piece of keen Wit; and such a one as any of my Sister Writers themselves would have been glad to have sent you. If it be the latter, I am still better pleased, as his own Account of himself fully confirms all that any of the Sisterhood, even the severest of them, have writ, or can ever write, upon that Topick. Therefore I would persuade my Sisters to use him with all imaginable Civility and Tenderness; for if I myself were to enter into a Controversy where more than two were to engage, I would certainly choose the Opposition of a weak Adversary, rather than the Assistance of a weak Friend. As for his Lady, (he may, for what I know, be a very Termagant, and such a Wife as would make even a wise Man uneasy. I neither acquit, nor condemn her, because I am not a proper Judge of the Case, having as yet heard but one of the Parties. All that I would contend for is, that the Fault of the Lady's Behaviour may not be laid to her Books; if they have innocently and undesignedly made her Company troublesome to her Husband, it can be for no other Reason but because she began to read too late. For if she had read half as much when she was single, as she seems inclined to do now (he is married, she would never have taken an illiterate Fox-hunting Squire for her Lord and Master). But still the poor Lady may not be to blame! Perhaps the harmless Girl was taken, by her indulgent Parents from a Boarding School, to be given to a Husband whom they supposed must make a good one, for no other Reason but because they had known his Father and Mother, many Years, for honest worthy People; and the young Squire was good natured, but that was only because none about him durst take the Liberty of displeasing him. For the fond

---

67 "She then desired his Permission to serve a Lady of Quality, by which Means she hoped to be able to provide for their two Children. But he refused it, unless he might have leave to visit her, when he pleased; *Hardships,* p. 31.

"But behold! the Sufferings which an Husband may inflict upon his Free-born *English* Wife, if he so please;" *Hardships,* p. 31.

Parents thought it better to neglect his Education, than his Health and to suffer his Understanding to become weakly and awry, rather than cross his Humour or spoil his Limbs; upon the same Principle, they laughed and diverted themselves at his Horse-play with Miss *Betty*, in the Christmas Holidays; and seeing her a pretty Girl, likely, to make a good fine Woman, and being a Neighbour's Child beside, wisely enough thought they could not better provide for the future Safety and Happiness of their Darling, than by making up a Match between the two Favourites. But the Squire at length coming to Years of maturity, instead of Discretion, has already been married long enough, to be tired of his Wife; he now thinks his Running Mare a much handsomer Creature,[68] and prefers the yelping of a Hound before her talk; especially if she is so unlucky as to speak Sense. In this unhappy Situation what can be done? To reconcile them to one another is as impossible as to reconcile Light and Darkness, Wit and Folly, Sense and no Sense; But since this can't be, let them try to reconcile themselves to themselves and to their own Condition. When the Gentleman mounts his Horse for the Field, let the Lady, repair (after having given the necessary Directions to her Servants about her Family Affairs) to her new Study, **[next page]** and read Lessons of Patience and Obedience, which may help to make her receive him with good Humour at Dinner-time; there let her look cheerful and pleased with all he says, till the Wine has railed the Spirits and Voices of himself and Companions to a proper Pitch for rehearsing the Musick of the Hounds and Horn; after which she may assemble her Neighbours, her Children, or her Maids, rather than want Company to make up a Concert, and sing over all the old Songs that ever her Nurse, or her Grandmother taught her, and so drown one Noise with another. But if her Temper inclines more to Silence and Solitude, let her retreat to the farthest Part of her House, or Garden, and amuse her self with walking, working, drawing, or any other innocent Entertainment, till the Squire's Mirth is at the full Height; which is common when one, or more, of the Company, are under the Table. After which, if it be in her Power, let her see him safe to his Bed; and then I seriously think, she has performed all the Matrimonial Duty, such a Husband can expect;[69] and may with quiet

---

68 "But suppose a Woman does not look upon Marriage as a common Bargain, and does not chuse to be barter'd for like a Horse or a Cow, she may chance to consider it as a religious Institution, and not as a civil Ordinance," [Mar. 1752] Mrs. Chapone N. d., but answers *FM XII, 2, ff.* to SR his March 2, 1752 and pp. 46–7 answered (after a delay) April 18.
69 "My Husband and I are both so apprehensive of the reigning Impiety of the Age, that we dare not trust our Children from us, and therefore educate them ourselves; I

Conscience at least, (whatever uneasy Sentiments may disturb her Heart) retire to her more agreeable Company, that I hope by this Time, are placed upon her Shelves; where she may enjoy herself and them, till Sleep, the kind Relief that Nature has provided for all our Day-time Cares, invites her to her Apartment; where I will leave her, and return to give one Word of Advice to the Squire, which is this; that if his Income, and his Expences, are so exactly even, that he cannot afford a supernumerary Servant, in the room of his Wife; that he would be pleased to turn off one Groom, two hunting Horses, and three couple of Hounds; and then I would venture to promise, that he should have the best House-keeper in England; and be a saver at the Year's End.[70] Yet, notwithstanding all that I have said, or more that I could say, I would have his Wife carefully inspect into the Behaviour of the Family, and likewise into their Accounts; for I fancy the Squire himself is not over intimate with Figures; but, beyond this I see no Reason or Occasion that can oblige a Woman of Fortune, and Fashion, to spend her Life in the Employment of a hired Servant, and divide her whole Time between her Kitchin, and her Home-stead; amongst her Plowmen, or her Hogs; unless it be an Employment she chooses, and then I have no more to say. Now Sir, to make some Atonement for the Freedoms I have taken in this Epistle, I beg you to believe me to be, with real Respect,

Your humble Servant,
DELIA.

N.B. In Compliance with this Correspondent's Request, I must assure her, that the two Ladies whom I had in my Thoughts were the *grave* Lady, whose Letter was printed together with one of my own in the same Paper, and *Somebody* who answer'd *Nobody*. This is all the Account 1 am capable of giving of them.

R. H.

---

assist as far as I am capable, which, together with the necessary Affairs of the Family, engrosses all my Time. If I have any Merit, it is in cheerfully quitting my *Book* and my *Pen*, for the *Needle* and *Distaff*, and endeavouring to do my Duty in that humble State of Life in which it has pleased GOD to place me. Far from assuming the Province of Direction, I am sufficiently happy if I can make my slender Abilities of any use to my Husband, to whose generous Spirit I owe the Improvements of them, and who has therefore all imaginable Right to claim their Application to his Ease and Service." Chapone's reply to Webster's invitation to contribute to the *WM*. See No. 243 (August 19, 1737).

70 "Women were designed for *Domestick Animals*, 'tis but allotting them their proper Place; give them *Needles* and *Prayer Books* there, and there's no great harm done." *Hardships*, p. 32. Case study here resembles cases in *Hardships* of failed marriages.

14. *Weekly Miscellany*, No. CCXCIX (299). Friday, September 15, 1738[71]

To DELIA.

MADAM,

My happy Intimacy with Mr. *Hooker* hath procured me the Pleasure of reading the *Copy* of a Letter with your Name at the Bottom.[72] I was so much pleased with the Performance, and so charm'd[73] with the Religious Zeal[74] of its Author, that I immediately determin'd to give the World some Intimation of what it has lost in the Concealment of a Letter[75] adorn'd with such Beauty of Stile and Honesty of Sentiment. No one would have been surpriz'd at its being a Woman's Production, who would have given himself Time to recollect the natural Genius of that Sex, its readiness and expertness to take every thing it is suffer'd to learn.[76] I have often lamented the Disadvantages Ladies lie under in that respect, and how seldom they are permitted any Acquaintance but with the Needle, or Pincushion; or are favour'd with any Communications but from the Governess, or Teacher. In that fine Mould Nature has cast her greatest Delicacies; and tho' thus denied the liberal Improvements of Men, some of them have crept out of their Bounds and Province of Embroidery and Plainwork, and have exhibited ingenious Pieces to entertain the Mind, as well as fine Shaded Works to feast the Sight. If I had not directed my Letter to *Delia*, I might have had an Opportunity to give her as a Proof of my Position. But to proceed on the Letter which troubles you with my Correspondence. The present Situation of Mr *Hooker's* Affairs, had he made no Excuse at all, must have satisfy'd you, on Recollection, as to its Disappearance in *Publick*. I own it is

---

71 This is apparently Richardson's first public letter to Sarah Chapone while encouraging her to contribute to the *Weekly Miscellany*.
72 Richardson publicly acknowledges his close relationship with Webster in producing the *Weekly Miscellany*.
73 "I am charmed with your Definition of Simplicity; and the Distinction you make in its Favour over Sincerity is worthy of Mrs. Chapone." Carroll, *Selected Letters*, p. 210.
74 "You know him to be a man of probity, of piety. He is a zealous Catholic; and you must allow, that a religious zeal is a strengthener, a confirmer, of all the social sanctions." *Sir Charles Grandison*, 3rd ed. (1754), Vol. VI. p. 91.
75 See Introduction, footnote 27.
76 "What a prodigy of learning, in the short reign of Edward the VIth, was the Lady Jane Grey! — Greek, as well as Latin, was familiar to her: So it was to Queen Elizabeth. And can it be supposed, that the natural genius's of those Ladies were more confined, or limited, for their knowledge of Latin and Greek? Milton, tho' a little nearer us, lived in harsher and more tumultuous times." *Sir Charles Grandison*, 7 vols. (1754), 3rd ed., Vol. VI, p. 358.

very hard that his Readers should be Sufferers, and loose [*sic*] any Entertainment because Truth is sometimes unseasonable and if Prudence ever deserves Censure, it is in a Case of this Nature. One Part of your Letter it seems his Modesty prevented him from publishing; I think he should have obliged us with that *by way of Curiosity;* Encomiums and civil Things that Gentleman has not, of late, been much troubled with. Upon the whole, tho' it suffers a Concealment, and like a hoarded Rarity is only produced to particular Intimates, tho' the World in general must want the Pleasure of seeing it, yet I will not deny myself that of congratulating you upon your noble Principle of Religion, upon the happy turn of Thought and Inclination which in an Age as vain and trifling, as it is loose and Irreligious, can prevail on you to correspond with the grave Mr. *Hooker,* and join in a Subject so necessary and important; a Subject which so few of your Sex, however qualify'd, endeavour to understand, or to relish. As some Old Fashions are daily reviv'd, I am sorry the Principles and Practices of some *Female Ancients* are no more imitated. Both Sacred and Prophane History give us the pleasing View of *Women* famed and illustrious for Piety and Virtue. The Faith and Courage of some have preserved Nations, and poor churlish *Nabal* is a remarkable Instance of the Benefit arising from marrying a *wise* and *good Woman.*[77] However incapable you may be thought, or however out of your Sphere it may be reckon'd, the World will be ever oblig'd to you, and, bad as it is, register with Honour **[middle column]** the fine Attempts (like yours) of any Female Advocate for Religion. 1 would not have you think your self quite singular, or that Mr. *Hooker* is alone in such a correspondent. I am happy in a like Instance; and when you have read the following Account of my Acquaintance, I am persuaded you'll approve her Sentiments and Conduct, and be as ready to congratulate me, as I have, my Friend *Hooker.* The Lady I mean is an agreeable Exception to the Rule which Women too generally lay down for themselves, of running into all the Modes of Folly and Vanity, to gain a little Cringing and Chattering which, they injudiciously construe Love and Admiration: But my Friend's Retinue of Admirers consists of Men with finer *Sense* than *Coats.* No Fool, nor Coxcomb is in her String of Lovers, and you are more likely to see her Picture in a wise Man's Study, than in a Fop's Snuff Box. If you visit her Closet you'll find more Books than Perfumes, no *untouch'd* Bible (to vary from the Poet) *disgraces* her Toilet and she

---

77 Abigail, Nabal's wife, saved his family from destruction by David after his "Churlishness." See "LIII. NABAL'S *Churlishness," A Compendious History of the Old and New Testament, extracted from the Holy Bible* (London, 1726), p. D 2. Not in Maslen, but apparently printed by Richardson. Ornaments R064, R450, and R360. Once again we are reminded that Richardson's printing shop was also a virtual library. Samuel Johnson had good reason to stay friends with this prosperous printer, *pace* Boswell.

lets no Pleasure divert her from her Duty.[78] Her Glass does not feed her Vanity whilst it reflects her Beauty; if she sees any Feature exact, and to be admired, it leads her to glorify her kind and great Creator. She contemns and laughs at the Rake, who snuffles out his Prophaness [sic] and Infidelity, and has no better Reason to defend his loose Opinion than that it is polite and fashionable. As she esteems her God her Friend, so she resents any Affront to him in her Company, and by that means weeds Conversation of all Ribaldry and Blasphemy. She takes more Pleasure in reading Men,[79] than looking at them, and is more delighted with a well-drawn Character than a *French* Pattern of Embroidery. I would not have you think my Friend is either a Prude or a *Female* Philosopher, her Conversation is as easy and facetious, as her Imagination is quick and sprightly. She confines her Reading to her Capacity, and never makes her self ridiculous by wading out of her Depth, and then sticking in the miry Problems. She has Gaiety without Coquetry, and you never see her in the whimsical Habits or Notions of young Fellows. She will no more put off the Dress than the native Modesty of her Sex, and is never seen *en Cavalier* at *Reviews* or *Horse-Races*. She is averse to all affected Airs, and Gestures; when she walks, you perceive an easy graceful Motion, without that *Tottering* and *genteel Hobling* which brings the poor Dancing-Master into Disgrace, and is besides a foolish mimicking of Lameness and Infirmity, which every one should confess her Obligations in being freed from. Her Virtues make Converts, as well as her Face Conquests; and whenever she enters a publick Place, like a drawn Sword she thins it of all empty Smarts and Flutterers. Beyond all this she goes constantly to her Parish Church, and behaves there with a *Beauty of Holiness*. She never laughs at the Parson or his Doctrine with her giggling Pew-Fellows, and nothing utter'd there produceth an unseemly Gesture. She considers the Church as the Place where her God has said *his Name shall be there*,[80] and is aw'd by that Consideration into Gravity and Decency. Her Eyes and her Heart are properly engag'd. All her Deportment

---

78 Explicit moral contrast to Pope's mock-epic heroine in *The Rape of a Lock*, already stereotyped by William Law. See *WM*, No.169 (March 6, 1736).

79 "Thou thyself art an adept in the pretended science of reading men; and, whenever thou art out, wilt study to find some reasons why it was more probable that thou shouldst have been right; and wilt watch every motion and action, and every word and sentiment, in the person thou hast once censured, for proofs, in order to help thee to revive and maintain thy first opinion. And, indeed, as thou seldom errest on the *favourable side*, human nature is so vile a thing, that thou art likely to be right five times in six, on the *other*: And perhaps it is but guessing of others, by what thou findest in thy own heart, to have reason to compliment thyself on thy penetration." Lovelace to John Belford, *Clarissa*, 3rd edn. (1751), Vol. 7, p. 9.

80 *Revelation* 22: 4.

is the Result of real unaffected Religion. As it has shewn her St. *Paul's more excellent Way*, so she keeps in it, and in every Station and Circumstance she acts upon that Prin- **[right column]** ciple, which never *behaves it self unseemly*. As Nature has given me an Eye to behold such a Woman with great Satisfaction, so I have another which streams for the Foibles of a ridiculous Contrast. Men for their own Sakes should prefer such Virtue to a transient Complexion. How well and exactly would the relative Duties of Life be perform'd were that beauteous Part of the Creation more serious and recollecting. *Religion* would give them fresh Beauty, and gain them wise Admirers, tho' it might not croud their Levees with Foppery and Nonsense. It would make fine young Ladies ripen into sober discreet Wives, and the Fruit appear as lovely in Maturity, as it is charming in its Bloom. Christian Graces and Virtues are always improving, 'till the fair Object of our Love becomes every Day more endearing and engaging, 'till the too often short-liv'd Passion is improved by her Behaviour into settled Friendship and Affection. The Speeches of a Lover, like the Beauty that ensnares him, are fading and transitory. An Author, I have somewhere met with, speaking of Courtship, thus expresses himself; "he ravisheth the Lilly of her Whiteness to colour her Face, and steals the Blushes of Roses to imbellish her Cheeks, he dims the Glittering of the Stars to increase the Brightness of her Eyes, and to hear him speak of her. Nature hath nothing wonderful which is not summ'd up in her Person; he resembles those Idols, which have Eyes and see not, and there may be notable Defects but Love is too blind to perceive them; altho' his Sight be continually fix'd upon her, he cannot discern her Spots from her Perfections,"[81] But all the Form and Regularity of the Entertainment is disorder'd after Grace is said. The Husband has other Eyes, other Affections; his Sight grows stronger than the Lover's, and he then *sees through* what before he only *looked at*. 'Tis then that *Religion* will prove it self the Pedestal of her Happiness; and when all those Lillies and Roses are faded, or grown contemptible by Familiarity, then the Behaviour which *Religion*

---

81 *Man without Passion: Or, The Wise STOICK, According to the SENTIMENTS OF SENECA.* Written originally in *French*, by that great and learned Philosopher, *ANTHONY LE GRAND*. Englished by *G. R. LONDON*, printed for *C. Harper*, and *J. Amery*, and sold by them at the *Flower de Luce*, and at the *Peacock*, both against St. *Dunstan*'s Church in *Fleet-street*. 1675, p. 142.] See reference to Seneca in *Pamela*, 6th ed. (1740), Vol. 3, p. 109. As Maslen has demonstrated, Richardson printed this source from Seneca.

 Maslen, p. 754: Seneca, Lucius Annaeus, *Select epistles on several moral subjects. Newly translated [...] By a Gentleman of Christ-Church, Oxon.* For C. Rivington, 1739;Maslen, p. 755: Seneca, Lucius Annaeus, *Select Epistles on Several Moral Subjects. Newly translated [...] By a Gentleman of Christ Church, Oxon.* Part II. For C. Rivington, 1740.

dictates will light up new Flames and fresh Affections; as a Wife, a Mother, and a Mistress, she'll receive the greatest Benefit and Character from a religious and virtuous Education and Habit; with her other Ornaments she'll have the Scripture one of a *meek* and *quiet* Spirit, and Religion will erect such a Fort of Virtues and good Qualities, as will secure her, in all probability, from ill Usage and those domestick Evils which compose the melancholy Catalogue of Matrimonial Misfortunes. In short, however the Face be featured, such a Woman cannot want Beauty, since she will have the Blush of Modesty and the White of Innocence to make her lovely and agreeable. There is no Folly nor Indiscretion against which *Religion* has not its Preservative. By a Daughter's being fixed and riveted [sic] in Principles which lead to honouring and obeying Parents, a Family has the best Security against unconsider'd and unadvised Marriages; so that take Life in what View you please, the greatest Advantage proceeds from *Religion*, from all Levities and Vanities the beauteous Sex would thereby be free, and the Beauty of the Mind no longer give ground to the perishable Beauty of the Body. As I am too old for a Lover, I wish the Ladies may accept my Service as a Tutor, and follow those Precepts which, more than any Fortune, will contribute to their Felicity. A **[next page]** Woman may with greater Justice be called an *Angel* when she resembles one in Purity and Innocence.[82]

May you, Madam, continue your wise Choice of a Correspondent tho' he is a Friend to Religion, and have a just Contempt of all Sneers and Ridicules whilst you are serving the noblest and best Cause, and promoting your Fellow Creatures' present and eternal Happiness.

I am, Yours, &c.

happy Intimacy 1/1 in *ECF.*

religious zeal 4/6

Case of this Nature 1/1

Principle of Religion 1/3

---

[82] "As far as is consistent with human frailty, and as far as she could be perfect, considering the people she had to deal with, and those with whom she was inseparably connected, she *is* perfect. To have been impeccable, must have left nothing for the Divine Grace and a Purified State to do, and carried our idea of her from woman to angel. As such is she often esteemed by the man whose *heart* was so corrupt, that he could hardly believe human nature capable of the purity, which, on every trial or temptation, shone out in *hers*." "Preface," *Clarissa*, 3rd ed. (1751), Vol. I, p. vii.

turn of Thought 1/3

miry   4/5

Modesty of her Sex   1 /2

Hobling 1 /2

unseemly 1/3

ripen into   4/6

Blush of Modesty   1/1

15. *Weekly Miscellany*, No. CCCII (302). Friday, October 6, 1738

Mr. Hooker,

Your gentle Readers, the *Female* ones especially, are desired to divest themselves of Prejudice; to forget, for the present, they are Inhabitants of *Cheapside*, or *Westminster*; to step back some thousands of Years, and to allow, there may be as great a Change of Manners, in such a length of Time, as of Cloaths, which formerly fitted every Body, and were a standing Treasury of Princes. I shou'd not doubt their relish of the following Piece, if they were learned enough to read the Translation of *Homer* with Taste, or good enough to read their *Bible* with Veneration: They will there find Princesses attending the Wardrobe, the Loom, and the washing their Linen; a beautiful Daughter of a wealthy Family drawing Water for the Flocks; the Wife of a Patriarch making Cakes on the Hearth and dressing savoury Meat for her Husband: And therefore will not much wonder at this *Matrimonial Dialogue* between a new married Couple. The Thing, indeed, is in itself very surprising: A Woman of Condition, scarce Fifteen, and a Bride, patiently sits by the Hour together to be school'd and tutor'd in the Duty of her Station by one, who pass'd for the best natured, most virtuous and prudent Man in *Athens*, the politest City of the World; near which he lived enjoying and improving his Family Estate: But then, *Ladies*, this happen'd above two thousand Years ago, before the Appellation, I now use to you, was known; when Women and Wives, like Horses, and Cows,[83] were call'd by their proper Names; before *Madam* and

---

83 "But suppose a Woman does not look upon Marriage as a common Bargain, and does not chuse to be barter'd for like a Horse or a Cow, she may chance to consider it as a religious Institution, and not as a civil Ordinance, and that her Compliance with the civil Ordinance is chiefly declaratory of her <inward> Resolution, that by the Grace

Sir made Parts of civil Speech; long before Quadrille, Dress, Tea and Visits became the whole Business of Life; and when the finest of your Sex thought it not beneath them to be good for something. I know, the oddness of the Thing raises your Curiosity, and you are impatient to hear what this old-fashion'd Spark said on the Occasion, and I hasten to gratify you with the Substance of it.

The first Thing he did, after the necessary Ceremonies and Endearments were over, was, to make the young Creature go down on her Knees and join with him in Prayers, that the Gods wou'd enable them to perform in a proper Manner each the Duties of their respective Stations. In a little Time after he began (like a Clown as you will call him.)

"*Wife*, have you ever considered for what Purposes I accepted, and your Parents bestow'd you on me? For, I presume, you cannot be ignorant that it was not for want of Choice of many others of Condition, with whom I might pass my Nights and Days: But, I suppose, we both, desirous of getting the best Partner of Life, expected to find such an one in each other. As to Children, if Heaven grants any, we will hereafter deliberate on the best way of their Education: For I conceive, we shall both find our Account in looking for the best Supports of Age in our Offspring. As to your *Person*, be so good to yourself and me, as not to use any other Embellishments, besides those honest and lasting ones of Cleanliness and Exercise: Do not affect to appear taller, or whiter, or redder, **[middle column]** than you really are; the Cheat cannot pass upon a *Husband*, who will see you at all Times; 'tis like *counterfeit Money* or *Affection*, which you wou'd blame him for putting off upon you, instead of true: Believe me, as Horses, Oxen and Sheep are most delightful to one another in their natural Hue and Figure, so are human Creatures to human. This Family Estate is our joint Possession: I have thrown all my Fortunes, and you yours into it, as a common Treasury: It is impertinent to consider, who has contributed most: The Person, who brings to it most Virtue and Oeconomy, will be allow'd to have brought the most valuable Stock.—*But what can my little Abilities do towards the common Work, since every Thing is in you and depends upon you? My Task is to be modest and frugal, if my Mother was right in her Instruction.*—As to that Point, my Instructions from my Father were the same: But good Men and Women may both so act, that their Possessions may be in the best Situation, and Increase arise out of sedulous and just Measures.—*But what, I beg, can I do to the Improvement of your Estate?*—Much, if you will execute in the best manner,

---

of God will perform all Duties required of her by **[new leaf: 145/8]** this religious Institution." Sarah Chapone to SR, *FM, XII,* 2, no date, but answers his letter of March 1, 1752.

what the Gods have enabled you to do, and the Customs of your Country have recommended to your Practice.—*And what are these Things?*—Not of the least Importance, I trow, unless the Female Leader of the *Bees* is employ'd in Affairs of little Consequence to the Hive. Heaven, with great Discernment, seems to have constituted this Pair, which we call *Male* and *Female*, that it might be most useful. First, that there may not be a Deficiency of this Species of Animals, they are joined together, in order to produce them; and hence Men have the power of providing the proper Supports of their Age and Infirmities. In the next place they do not live abroad in open Air, like the other Animals, but have occasion for shelter in covered Houses. Those who wou'd have Necessaries to import into these Habitations, must have some to attend the Works of the Country and Fields without Doors: For ploughing, sowing, planting and pasture, are without-door Works, and of these come the Necessaries of Life. When these are brought under Cover, there will be wanting one to place them in proper Repositories and preserve and work them up for the use of the Family. Under Cover must be the Education of the Offspring,[84] the Confection of the imported Fruits of the Earth, and the Manufacture of Linen and Wool for cloathing. Since both these sorts of Works without and within Doors call for Care and Inspection, God has, in my Opinion, provided for both, by framing the Nature of *Women* for the domestic Labours and Cares, and that of *Men* for those abroad: For he has fitted the Body and Mind of *Man* so as best to encounter Cold and Heat, the fatigue of Journeys and Dangers of War, and by that fitness enjoin'd him his Task without Doors: But the *Woman's* Constitution, being more delicate and less patient of Labour, recommends to her the Province within the House. As part of this Province is to breed up the tender Offspring, the Supreme Power has not only commanded her to **[right column]** do it, but framed her for it, by giving her more fondness for her Children, than to the other Parent:[85] And as her Business is to keep what is imported into the House, the same Providence has excellently qualify'd her for it, by giving to her a greater

---

84 The Chapones educated their children at home.
85 "But in the human Species paternal and maternal Care and Affection are found in [18] Nature to be both strong and active; but I believe it will be readily allow'd me that it is in general more so in the Mother. One would therefore suppose that the Mother is in some Degree qualified, as she is more inclined by Nature, to take Care of the Children. In the Levitical Law, we see the Evidence of both Parents necessary, to the Conviction and Punishment of a rebellious Son. We are also told in the sacred Pages that, God has confirmed Authority of the Mother over the Sons. We can't therefore but conclude that God well knew that he had qualified her to give Laws, when he so strictly enjoins the Observation of them," *Hardships,* p. 34.

degree of careful Fear and Apprehension, than to the *Man*; as it has given him more Strength and Courage, in order to ward off external Violence. But as it is common to both to give out and receive, and consequently to keep Accompts, to both are given in common Memory and Diligence, that you cannot say, which by Nature has most. Continence and Temperance are indulged alike to both, and it is in the power of either to be better, if the Endeavours after it are greater in one, than the other. As you see each Sex has its different Endowments fitted for the different Works of Life, for this Cause they want each other's Assistance, and the Union increases the Utility, one supplying what the other is deficient in. Apprised of this wise Distribution of things from above, we must attend and adorn our respective Employments. The Customs and Constitutions of all civilized Nations conspire with the Voice of God and Nature, making Men and Women joint Partners of the Children and Family, and stamp a Credit on them for doing, what they are best qualify'd to do. It is the Point of Commendation in one Sex to stay within and not gad abroad, and a Disgrace to the other to do so, to the neglect of what is abroad: And if any one contradicts this Order of Nature and Appointment of his Country, it is no Secret to the all-seeing Eye, and he is punish'd and grows ridiculous, for omitting his own Works and perversely invading those of another. The *Queen* of the *Bees* seems to be a perfect Example of doing the Business imposed upon her by Providence. — *And what, pray, are those Works, which she does for my Imitation?* — Why, she, staying at home in the Hive, suffers not the Bees to be idle; She sends out those that are proper to work and receives, disposes and preserves, what each of them brings, and at the Time of using them, distributes to every one his proper Portion; she presides within over the Works of the Combs, and sees they are built and stored with Diligence and Accuracy; takes care of the Offspring, and when they are able to take the Wing for Labour, sends them out to some new Colony, under a discreet Leader of their own. There is so near an Affinity in all this to your Affairs, that you cannot help discerning it to be your Province to send out some to superintend the Works of others; if you know more, to teach; if less, to learn; to distribute what is brought in or present Consumption, and lay up what is to be kept for the future Necessities of the Year. And this Disposition of these things for Use will be the easiest matter in the World, if you will observe Order, which makes an Army of a Rabble, gives Beauty to the richest Furniture, and adds Grace even to such mean Utensils and Pans, when they are placed in their proper Offices under a due Arrangement, [*sic*, words missing] ing and the Preparation of the Victuals directly under your Care. The very **[word concealed by stamp]**

[verso]

necessary for the Inspection of these Particulars, will at once be an Exercise of Health, and an Amusement of Pleasure, and your personal Labour and Bustle in some of them will make your Meals more grateful, give Vigour to your Constitution, and Colour to your Complexion. One part of your Employment may perhaps be disagreeable to you, which is to attend and recover proper Care and Tenderness those of your Family, who may be sick or hurt: But then the Return is proportionably great; for it is by such kind and amiable Offices of the *Regent* of the *Hive*, that the *Bees* are all so attached to her, that they follow her wherever she leads, and if she quits the Hive, not a Creature stays behind, or is seen out of her Retinue.— *You tell me Wonders of this winged Queen; but it is marvelous to me, if the Affair of Government does not belong to you, rather than me; for my Care and Distribution wou'd have no Place within, if you did not take care to send in from without, what I am to employ myself upon.*— I am sure ridiculous and useless wou'd be my Care of importing, if there was not one to overlook the Things imported: The Case would be that pityable one of drawing into a perforated Vessel, which you know, is losing one's Labour. And to make amends for the painful Parts of your Employment, some of your Cares will carry their Reward of Pleasure along with them, as when you receive a Servant ignorant of Female Works, and you make her expert, and turn an unexperienced Housekeeper into a skillful, diligent and faithful one of any Value: *Sovereignty* must be delightful, which you will insensibly acquire, while you distribute your Favours and Rewards to the sober and useful Members of your Family, and punish with discreet Severities, if any one, under such Examples, be otherwise. But the sweetest of all is, that if you appear better in your Province, than I in mine, you will have me among the Servants, who love and respect you. Nor need you apprehend, the advance of Age, or decay of Face, will cool Affection, or diminish Esteem: The older you are the more honour'd you will be in proportion to your successful Care of me, your Children, and Family. For Goodness is for ever lovely, and Virtue fixes the Charms of Person and gives Eternity to Beauty."

It is said, (wou'd you believe it?) this extraordinary young Female rose up from this serious Lecture, enamour'd of the Person who gave it, flush'd with joy at the Confidence reposed in her, and fired with Ambition to deserve and exceed it, and became the most notable, prudent, and agreeable Wife of her Age and Country.

I scarce dare imagine to myself, how a modern Lady, under all the Lights and Advantages of the present Education, wou'd have behaved on the like Occasion. She wou'd not, it is probable, have been the *Hearer* only, and been contented to drop a Courtesy, and put in a Word now and then to shew her Attention. She might have fired at the mention of *Consideration,* and said, she left it to those plodding Folks, who valued themselves upon it; that it was long since she had learn'd her *Catechism,* or play'd at *Questions* and *Commands*; but, however, that Flesh and Blood cou'd not help replying to some of his odd Enquiries and Observations: That she did not apprehend, what he meant by his common Stock, and his civil Intimation of the Choice he had of other Ladies; that, as she was conscious of her own Charms, the wonder lay on the other side, what, beside her evil Stars, cou'd induce her to do him the Favour; and as she very well remembered what Fortune she brought, she expected *her Pin-money*[86] shou'd be duely paid, and her *separate Maintenance,* if there was occasion for it. In the midst of his sagacious Directions about the Use and Pleasure of *Oeconomy* and Household Affairs, she might have briskly rung her Bell, and call'd **[right column]** up for her Cook, her Butler and Laundry-Maid, and told them, their Master was in a Humour of giving some excellent Lessons, which might be of Use to them, and therefore it was pity they, should be lost: And then in their Presence said, that her Ambition rose much higher than to the Dominion over Cattle and Slaves and a Husband, and the delightful Employments of making Pastry, listening to the cackling of a Hen, or tinkling the Warming-Pan[87] to a swarm of Bees:[88] That in short, she insisted upon going immediately to her House at *Athens,* and hoped to make Conquests of another Nature in gay Assemblies and crowded Theatres; and promised herself more Entertainment from one merry Scene of *Aristophanes,* than from all the grave impertinent stuff in the School of *Socrates* or his Disciples.— At the instant the Coach might have been call'd for, and the good Man left to read a Lecture of Patience to himself.

It is lucky for me, that I have nothing more to say, at the very Time when I perceive I have said enough to fill your Paper, and give me an Opportunity of subscribing myself.

Yours etc.,

AGRICOLA.

---

86 "1.1674– A (usually annual) sum allotted to a woman for clothing and other personal expenses; *esp.* such an allowance provided for a wife's private expenditure. Now *historical.*" OED.

87 "A long-handled covered pan of metal (usually of brass) to contain live coals, etc., formerly in common use for warming beds" *OED.*

88 "but, beyond this I see no Reason or Occasion that can oblige a Woman of Fortune, and Fashion, to spend her Life in the Employment of a hired Servant, and divide her whole Time between her Kitchin, and her Home-stead; amongst her Plowmen, or her Hogs; unless it be an Employment she chooses, and then I have no more to say." Delia, *WM,* No. 290 (July 14, 1738).

16. *Weekly Miscellany*, No. CCCIV (304). Saturday, October 21, 1738

I HAVE receiv'd a second Letter upon *Prudence,* which I did intend to have publish'd this Week, but my Correspondent must excuse me if I postpone it 'tis the next. I think myself so much honoured by this Lady's Correspondence, and my Readers are so much obliged to her, I should be wanting in my Regard to both if I did not always give her Place. None of our Sex will dispute it with her, tho' I wish some of her own would be her Rivals for it. Yet, as great as her Merit is, it is an Instance of Generosity as well as Justice in me to pay a due Respect to it. For, tho' she writes with a Spirit of Good-humour, she has insinuated the most severe Reflection upon my *Condition,* and added to the Misfortune of being an *Old Batchelor* by imputing it to me as a Crime. If the Lady intends to give me a modest Hint, before I can be the better for it she must give me another, for at present I neither know where she lives, nor who she is. If she means to reprove me for my past Conduct, or to shame me into a Matrimonial Intention, I desire to be heard a Word or two in my Defence. We *Old Batchelors,* when the Joke bears hard upon us, have a set of Excuses much older than our selves, and, as far as *Delia* knows, some one, or all of them may unhappily belong to me; so that before she sends evil Spirits to haunt my Chamber, and peep in at my Curtains, she should have some better Proof, than Conjecture, of my Guilt. But, however Criminal I have been as to my Conduct, be it known to *Delia,* and to all whom it may concern, that I am ready to change my *present* Condition, being pretty well assured that I cannot have the worst of the Bargain, unless the cross *old Maid* should unluckily fall to my Lot. The Difficulty, I fear, will be, to find out an agreeable Person *in her Senses* (and I should not care to turn *Mad Doctor,* and take a *Lunatick* for Life) who would make an *Hospital* of her self, for the *Support* of an *Invalid,* worn out with Fatigues, and almost past his Labour. The only Expedient I can think of for helping off such a poor Mortal was suggested to me by my Correspondent's Letter of last Week, and *Delia* is the fittest Person to put it in Execution. If I could any how get to be *Knighted,* my Life for her's, (and that is laying odds) I shall find some wealthy Tradesman,[89] as other Great Folks, have done before me, who will, gladly pay my Debts, and thank me for the *Favour* of making a *Lady* of his Daughter, let my Age, Behaviour, Character, or Temper be what it will. Now, the Business is done if *Delia* has but a Friend, or a Friend's Friend, at Court, or near the Court, and will recommend me heartily. If her Person be as persuasive as her Pen, she cannot ask in vain; and her Good-nature be equal to her Wit, I have hopes of her Assistance. She

---

89 Richardson as his patron!

speaks of her great Infirmities, which may possibly take her out of this wicked World before she has put me into it; but her *Interest* with those who know her can never die, because her Perfections can never be forgotten by them; and if she makes it her Request, it will have more Influence upon generous Minds than a living one.—If she succeeds in her Application, and obtains a *Promise*, I **[middle column]** should be glad, for several Reasons, to know it. I shall have the more Time to think of Ways and Means to raise Money to pay the Fees of my *Knighthood*, and provide a proper Equipage. It will give me new Spirits, and make me quite a young Man again. Besides, I shall be able to form to my self a Scheme of Life suitable to my new Dignity.

Some of my Readers will want mightily to know the Meaning of all this. I can assure them, it *has* a Meaning, which I hope will be understood by somebody, or another, and misunderstood by the rest, as they in their Discretion shall think fit.

R. H.

S I R,
I FIND my self under a sort of Necessity of assuring you and the Publick too, (if you think it worth while) that the enclosed, design'd for your Friend, was finished before I had seen your Paper of the 6th Instant, and only lay for a proper Opportunity of being conveyed to you. I tell you this, because it should not be supposed that I intended in the least to point at that Letter. Had I seen it before I writ, I should neither have animadverted upon, nor contradicted it, for I like the Narrative so well, that I wish with all my Heart, your Correspondent would procure a competent number of *Londoners*, as virtuous, and as reasonable, as his *Athenian*[90]; for I am satisfied, if he could do that, he would soon find that good Women are not quite so scarce as he at present imagines. I have Time to say no more but that I am,

Mr. Hooker's
Humble Servant.[91]

S I R,

YOU have drawn so amiable a Portraiture of your Woman Friend, that I esteem her as much as any of my old Acquaintance; and hope we shall soon

---

90 *Agricola*, the Athenian persona for Chapone's letter of *WM*, No. 302 (October 6, 1738).
91 Richardson probably wrote this note to make sure that Webster would publish Chapone's letter.

see her enter the Lists as a Voluntier [*sic*]. I have already destined her to be my Aide-de-Camp, and in due time my Successor; and do not doubt but that she will amply supply the Defects of a weak Head, and weaker Hand; two wretched Qualifications, I confess, (though my own) for writing to Mr. *Hooker's* Friend. But as Friends that never saw each other can converse with more Freedom than is generally proper with those we personally talk with; I shall go on to tell you, as Mr. *Hooker* likewise will confirm to you, that I am pretty well advanced in Years, naturally very fearful, and of late, excessively vapourish.[92] Now the first of these inclines one to be suspicious, the second to be afraid of every thing; and the last Foible makes us always fear the worst. This, all together, has raised a terrible Apprehension in my Mind, that this fine Lady (as you may think her) is one of those Aerial Spirits that delight in playing their unlucky Tricks amongst us poor Mortals;[93] upon which Design they sometimes haunt the Chamber of an old Maid in so frightful a Shape; that she is forced to take her Father's Coachman, or at best some pretended Gentleman, for a Guard. At other **[right column]** Times they peep in at the Curtains of some superannuated Batchelor, and put on a figure suited to the Life he has formerly led. If he has debauched innocent Creatures, with no other View than to gratify his own depraved Appetite; if he has made Love, for Years, to Women of Character and has left them when he found he could not gain his wicked Ends; with a thousand other nameless Crimes; then the artful Spirit appears in so terrible a manner as leaves him really troubled in Mind, and, it may be, sorry for his Faults, but without a possibility of ever repairing them. If he is one that has avoided Matrimony merely because he would not be at the Trouble and Expence of keeping a Wife and Children, the same Spirit who laughed at the Fears of the former can put on so beautiful and tempting an Appearance, that the old Gentleman rises in the Morning and falls in Love with his Maid and marries her, or perhaps, his

---

[92] "As I am an Old Woman, [Chapone is 52] and have never seen you, [Chapone never met Richardson as of 1752] Sir, I think I may venture to tell you, without being supposed to have in Mind to run away with you, that I am with the most rapid Affection Blessing to our Brown Maid

           Your most obliged and
           most obedient humble
              Servant
            Sarah Chapone"

N. d., but answers *FM XII*, 2, *ff.* to SR his March 2, 1752 and pp. 46–57 answered (after a delay) April 18.

[93] "Phantom of your own creating," see letter by Somebody, *WM*, No. 284 (June 2, 1738).

Barber's Daughter who happens that Day to bring home his Peruke; and then we may suppose, the Laugh is louder and more general. Now, I have so much Regard for every Friend of Mr. *Hooker's*, that as you have put yourself in the same Class with him and me in Point of Age, I cannot but warn you of your Danger, and acquaint you with my Fears; which are the stronger because I must own, that I do not know two real Women in the two Kingdoms that can in every Point come up to your Prescription; if I did, and your Friend were truly Flesh and Bone, I would propose to erect them into a Triumvirate cloathed with all the Authority that those of Old enjoyed, in order to see if it were possible to reform one half at least of Human-kind. But if she be of the other sort, I declare to you, without farther Ceremony, that I will have nothing to say to her, if I can help it. For of all things in this lower World, Witches, Spirits, and Apparitions, are what I dread the most: And, though I have read some elaborate Treatises to prove there is no such thing in Nature,[94] yet I cannot get over the Prejudices of Education, and the Nursery. Nay, so incurably silly am I, that the very Repealing Act itself has not made me one jot less credulous, nor less cowardly, than I was before it passed.[95] It is true, I can bear the sight of Metamorphoses and shifting of Shapes without the least Terror, because we are used to it at the Theatre. I have seen a grave elderly Gentleman turned into a sprightly young Lady, and a teazed provoked Man transformed into an easy happy Friend; but these are agreeable Changes, and such as give us only Surprise and Pleasure. That I am very much under the Moon's Influence (as the rest of my Sex are generally said to be) your Friend *H.* can inform you; but that you may not think me quite mad (for I am only a little tending that Way) I must assume a more serious Air, and tell you my Opinion, which is, that Mr. *Hooker* and you concur and seem to vie with each other who shall be the most complaisant to us.[96] And therefore, instead of reproaching us with our Faults and Follies, you have with the most refined and delicate kind of Flattery, set before our Eyes this fine Picture, not to shew us what we are, but what we ought to be; and what a Woman of Sense might really be, with a very little. And why Gentlemen deny it us is a Point that **[next page]** I have neither Time nor Patience to discuss. As to the lowest Rank of People, who are to live by the united Care and Pains of the Husband and Wife, Nature seems to have placed them so exactly upon a Level, that

---

94 For example, *A Discourse on Witchcraft. Occasioned by a bill now depending in Parliament, to repeal the statue made in the first year of the reign of King James I.* (1736).
95 A bill to repeal the statute made in the first year of the reign of King James I against witchcraft, 1736.
96 That is, Richardson and Webster have conspired to set the highest standard of womanhood.

in all my Observation there never was a Contention among such who had the most Sense, but the Well-being of the Family depended as much upon the Housewifery and good Management of the Woman, as on the Strength and laborious Industry of the Man.[97] And for those in the next Class, take a Man bred up at a common School, where he is taught to read and write and construe his *Latin* Grammar, and has the rest of his Education behind a Counter; let Chance or Providence throw a great Estate in his Way, what a despicable Figure does, he make? and what does he do with it? Why he can strut, and bluster, wear fine Cloaths, be imperious to his Servants, insolent to his Acquaintance, if their Fortune does not come up to his; as for those above him, he flies their Conversation, as conscious that he is not at all fit for it. Here, indeed, a Woman with one Degree of Learning above her Maid would be quite thrown away; for her better Understanding would only serve for a mutual Mortification, to her self, and her Husband. But why a Man with natural Good Sense of his own, improved by a liberal Education; should grudge a Woman the Pleasure of reading any thing besides Books of Cookery, and Receipts in Surgery and Physick, I never could guess.[98] Certainly such a one, however Fair she may be, can be no very agreeable Companion to a Man of Letters, (especially when Life's Meridian is past) who flares and starts when she hears a hard Word, as if she thought you were going to conjure up some evil Spirit;[99] or if an Author, or a Book is the Subject of Discourse, yawns and retires, for fear of falling asleep in the midst of the Company*. But after all my Reading, and my Writing too, I take it as undoubted, that Men, as Men, will do what they please;[100] and Women, as Women, must do as well as they can. Upon the whole, you and your Friend *have* been so complaisant to the Sex in general, and to me in particular, that I cannot but allow ye both to be

---

97 Marriage depends on wife's good housekeeping as well as upon the husband's physical strength and educational privileges: "And as her Business is to keep what is imported into the House, the same Providence has excellently qualify'd her for it, by giving to her a greater degree of careful Fear and Apprehension, than to the *Man*; as it has given him more Strength and Courage, in order to ward off external Violence," *WM*, No. 302 (October 6, 1738).
98 Same situation as in *WM*, No. 290 (July 14, 1738), on plight of educated wife with boorish husband.
99 Chapone's point that women were deliberately brought up to have imaginary fears to keep them timid and thus prepared for proper obeisance in marriage.
100 "But behold! the Sufferings which an Husband may inflict upon his Free-born *English* Wife, if he so please," *Hardships*, p. 31.

Exceptions to all I have ever writ; and therefore am with due Respect to him in the first Place,

Sir, your humble Servant,

D E L I A.

Some-body,

Any-body,

Or what you please to call me.[101]

* *I wish my Ingenious Correspondent well out of his miry Problems,*[102] *for he seems to be in more danger sticking there than the learned Lady. I leave him to stand, or fall, by his own Opinion. for I declare, mine to be, that a Wife will be, to a Man of Sense, the more prudent Friend, and the more agreeable Companion, the better Understanding and the more Knowledge she has.*

17. *Weekly Miscellany*, No. CCCLIII (353). Saturday, September 29, 1739

Letter from Belinda.

SIR,

If you turn over the Leaf, you'll see the Name of your old Correspondent; the sight of which, I suppose, will bring to your Remembrance a *Promise* of mine, made some time ago. I do acknowledge that I gave you some reason to expect a Letter from me, but the Disappointment could not be great, where the Thing expected was of so trifling a Nature, and the Person from whom you expected it no other than a giddy young Girl. It is very Unphilosophical to lay more Stress upon a Thing than the Nature of it will bear. In *former* Times, before Men had gone to the bottom of Things and seen thro' those *Appearances* which

---

101 Chapone as *Delia, Somebody, Agricola,* or *what you please.*
102 "She [Richardson's *Belinda*] confines her Reading to her Capacity, and never makes her self ridiculous by wading out of her Depth, and then sticking in the miry Problems. She has Gaiety without Coquetry, and you never see her in the whimsical Habits or Notions of young Fellows," *WM,* No. 299 (September 15, 1738). Chapone obviously took offense at the presumption that a woman could not cope with difficult analysis of ideas.

imposed upon superficial Searchers into moral Truths, *Oaths* and *Promises,* tho' to the *greatest hindrance* of the Person who made them, were esteem'd binding; but a *Promise* is really no more than a strong *Declaration* of our *Intention* at that Time, but carries no Obligation to the Performance of it, provided it should prove *Inconvenient.* This is a Maxim, in our Age of *Light* and *Knowledge,* so universally received by all Persons of any tolerable Share of *Shrewdness* and *Discretion,* that the profound Mr. *Hooker,* whatever he thinks, will be ashamed to dispute the Truth of it. Now, good Sir, for as much as my last Letter signify'd no more than that I did *purpose* in a short Time to send you another, it was your Fault if you put an *Old Sense* upon *Modern Words,* and by such an obsolete Signification raised false Expectations; and, since I could not be understood to do more than intimate a *Resolution,* it cannot seem strange to you that a *Woman,* and a Woman of my Age and Gaity, should change her Mind. Thus far, then, I stand; acquitted, as to any *Obligation* on *my* Side, or any *Injury* on *yours.* But, still, the Reasons for my not writing to you, as I intended, are not strictly justifiable; and, as I find, by your last *Miscellany,* that it is our Duty to make *Confession* of our Faults one to another, and to speak freely the *real State of our Hearts,* I shall *plainly* and *concisely* tell you the *Temptations* that prevail'd over me. In good Truth, my Reasons were no better than *Pride* and *Vanity,* which I allow to be great Faults, tho' not peculiar to our Sex. I was made to believe that my former Letters were in some degree of Credit with your Readers, and that *Belinda,* as Times go, was reckon'd a good smart, lively Girl, with some little Humour. Inquiry was made after me, and such as knew, or suspected me to be the Author, congratulated me upon it. This, you may be sure, was pleasing enough to our natural Desire of Praise, and excited an Ambition to add to the Reputation which I had acquired. But two Circumstances unfortunately conspired to check my aspiring Thoughts, and to frustrate my Views.—The superior Excellence and Success of a *Rival* is what no Person of any Spirit could ever bear with Temper, and I have been *rival'd* and *excell'd,* not only by one of my own Sex, but by my self. The first requires no Explanation; and the Second, like a *Riddle,* is very easy when explained. I need not tell you that *Delia* was my *Female* Rival, any more than I can deny the Superiority of her Genius and Performances. I was tolerably well pleased with my self while I looked in the flattering Glass of my *Letters* with the Eye of *Self-Love,* but when I saw, and could not help seeing so many more and so much more shining Beauties in *hers,* I was so much mortified and discouraged, I determined to write no more. If I had only seen the disagreeable Comparison in *private,* I might, possibly, by Degrees, and with the Assistance of my own Vanity, have view'd it with less Envy; but when I never could hear a civil Thing said of *Belinda,* but it gave Occasion to every one of an allowed Taste to run out into the most lavish Panegyrick on *Delia,* I was out of all Patience, and immediately invented some excuse for leaving the Company. Had her *bodily* Perfections been the Subject of their Praises, I could with less regret have yielded the Precedence to her, for as there are so many more of our Sex who can *look* than of those who can *write agreeably*, I pique my self more upon the Character of an *Author* than the Reputation of my *Beauty*, and could patiently have borne to hear your Sex agree in Opinion that *Delia* was a much finer *Woman* than *Belinda*, if they could not with so much Justice have added that, she was a better *Writer*. However, so high was my Opinion of the Usefulness of your Design, so sincere my Wishes for the Success of it, so strong my Persuasion that *Delia* was capable of adorning and recommending your Paper, my honest Zeal made me with you the continuance of *her* Correspondence, tho' my Pride obliged me to discontinue *my own*. But, now, I am doubly disappointed and doubly mortified. I have lost, not only the Pleasure of *Self-Conceit*, but the more generous Satisfaction of seeing the happy Fruits of successful Merit. When *Delia* had convinced your Readers that she could greatly excel *Belinda*, those Infirmities of Body of which she complained deprived the Publick of the Excellencies of her Mind; and you, Mr. *Hooker*, instead of gaining a better Correspondent, lost both. I impute her Silence to her Death, not only because she mention'd her ill state of Health, but because I am unwilling to imagine that she wrote only to shew that she could write better than her Neighbours, and wrote no longer than 'till she had answered that ungenerous End.

When *Delia* had been some Time dead, and the odious Comparison removed out of sight, I began to think of renewing my Correspondence with you, but by a Concurrence of Accidents it happened that my own Letters, that I had sent you formerly, became as great an Obstacle as *Delia's*; I found that I was as incapable of writing like *my self*, as I was of writing like *her*; and could no more bear the Thoughts of falling short of my own, however imperfect, Performances, than of being outdone by another. A Series of Trouble and Disappointments, with frequent Indispositions, have greatly affected my natural Temper, damp'd the Vivacity of my Spirits, and given a Turn to my Mind quite opposite to that Pleasantry which I had delighted to shew. In short, tho' the *Name* of *Belinda* was still living, the *Character* died, and probably by this Time is buried in Oblivion. Let its Memory rest undisturb'd by Envy and Ill-Nature, which I shall never again be able to revive by the Gaity and Good Humour of any future Compositions.—The Thoughts of being *Superannuated*, or, which **[right column]** is altogether as mortifying a Circumstance, of being *disabled* and *useless*, still added to my Chagreen. To live an idle Drone in Obscurity, like an Invalid in an Hospital, was a Life too insignificant for my Spirit to bear. From that Moment I resolved to be *Somebody*, tho' I could not be what I *had* been. Before my *Aunt* died she had obliged me, by the Force of her Authority, and by the greater Influence of her Example, to spend a great part of that Leisure which my Fortune gave me, in my Study, under the Direction of that venerable and worthy Man of whom I have given an Account in your Paper. I gave my self up wholly to *Retirement*; and endeavoured to find that Happiness in *Books* and *Contemplation* which I despaired of finding any where else; and by way of Improvement in Knowledge, as well as for the Amusement of my Thoughts, I have usually accustomed my self to write something every Day. This custom, I soon perceived, help'd greatly to enlarge my Stock of Ideas, and to range them in better Order; to clear my Apprehension of Things, and to settle my Judgment; to methodize and express my Thoughts with Readiness and Propriety. At first I was a good deal discouraged; for when I came to digest and examine my Sentiments, many proved erroneous, many imperfect; and after I had made my self Mistress of a Subject, it proved to be a great deal more difficult than I could have imagined, to communicate them to any Advantage. A right Order of the different Parts of a Composition, a close Connection, and an easy Transition from one to another, (from whence arises Perspicuity, the greatest Beauty in Writing) these are Perfections which the greatest Industry cannot acquire without the Gift of Nature, and which are usually as much beyond the reach of Nature without the Aids of habitual Exercise. I believe, there is nothing more difficult than to write with Accuracy and Elegancy, nothing of which there are fewer good Judges; and yet every one who barely understands the Meaning of the *Words* in which any Book is written will presume, without Examination, to pronounce authoritatively upon its *Defects*, or *Beauties*; which is as great an Absurdity as if an ignorant Clown should attempt to criticize upon the masterly Strokes of a *Raphael*, or a *Titian*; a *Vandyke*, or a *Kneller*.[103] But, let the Eye be ever so skilful and accustomed to good Paintings, tho' the Piece will appear beautiful at first Sight, it is impossible that *all* its Excellencies should shew themselves at one View; and some of them may be of so *nice* a Nature as to require a nearer Inspection. For these Reasons few Readers do Justice either to a *good* Writer, or a *bad* one. To find out the *Faults,* or *Perfections* of a Composition, requires more Knowledge and Judgment than fall to the Share of most of them, and more Attention than they will be at the trouble of giving. If this Observation be, as it is, a great Discouragement to many of your Correspondents, it gives great Comfort to such imperfect Writers as your humble Servant; who, in adventuring to become *Authors*, trust more to the *Ignorance* than to the *Candour* of the Publick; and adventure the more boldly because they have but little to lose. I have inadvertently deviated from the original Design of this Letter into Critical Remarks, which, perhaps, may be thought as much beyond my

---

103 See Introduction, p. 15, footnotes 32 and 33.

Sphere and Capacity. **[new page]** I intended, when I first took up my Pen, only to give you the Reason why you have not heard from me so long, and how it happens that I now appear in such a different Dress. I cannot, as I have done, undertake to make your Readers *laugh*, or so much as *smile*; but if I am grown less entertaining, I will endeavour to make some Amends by being as useful as I possibly can. If I have lost that little Share of *Wit* which some have been so complaisant as to ascribe to me, I have acquired what has more Merit, tho' it be not so apt to attract Admiration, or give Pleasure. Be that as it will, if you will insert what I intend to send you, and your Readers will have the Patience to peruse it, you may expect soon to hear from,

Your well-wisher,

Northamptonshire,
Sept. 20. 1739. BELINDA.

18. *Weekly Miscellany*, No. CCCLX (360). Saturday, November 17, 1739

Letter to Belinda from Delia.

To BELINDA.

If you can excuse Brevity and Delays, I have some Thoughts to communicate to you; which, as *Sancho* says, I must vent some Way or other, lest they should rot upon my Stomach, and make me worse than I am.[104] At the Time I first saw your extravagantly complaisant (not to say flattering) Letter, I had before me a Table covered with Cordials, Pills, Boluses, Tincture of Soot, &c. and, in a Word, all the Apparatus of an Apothecary's Shop; besides China Basons, Glasses, Tea Spoons, other Spoons and Sauce-pans: And behind me, that is at my own Back, a Blister,[105] much about the size of a square Trencher:[106] For I find these Gentlemen, though they resemble our travelled Taylors in the length of their Bills, yet have not, like them, the good Manners to come and take measure of one's Breadth; but graciously leave that part of the Work to their Friends and Followers, the Undertakers.

---

104 Miguel de Cervantes Saavedra, *The History of the most ingenious knight Don Quixote de la Mancha*, In Two Volumes (London, 1706), Vol. 1, p. 99.
105 "*Medicine*. Anything applied to raise a blister; a vesicatory." *OED*.
106 "A flat piece of wood, square or circular, on which meat was served and cut up; a plate or platter of wood, metal, or earthenware. *archaic* and *Historical*." *OED*.

Although I am the most risible Creature upon Earth, I have at the same time the most childish Weakness: So that I can without Vanity say, that I can laugh or cry with any Body in the Kingdom: and have sometimes had the secret Pleasure of seeing my serious Doctor kind Relations and diligent Attendants sympathizing with me, and playing the Fool almost as much as my self.

Now, I hope, *Belinda* will allow this to be a whimsical Situation for writing; especially to so ingenious a Lady. But as I am something better, and have little more to do, than to shrug up my Shoulders (like a heavy *Dutchman* that keeps both his Hands in his Pockets to secure his Money; or a gay *Frenchman*, that wisely and falsely talks Politicks out of his own Country, and feels in his Fob the while, to know whether he has any of that cumbersome Metal about him) I resolved to take the Opportunity to make *Belinda* easy;[107] and to let her know, in an authentic Manner, that I intirely resign to her all Right, Claim, or Pretension whatsoever to the Empire of Love and Wit. You, by your own Account, are young, and may hope for the Recovery of your Health, and a long successful Reign.

You pretend to make me believe, that I have rival'd you in Writing. But this is an Uncertainty, and cannot be decided by you or me; but must be left to the Judgment, not to say the Fancy, of the Reader. But sure I am that you have out-rival'd me in the 'Squire's Affections. I plainly see you have gained his Heart; so that I may say with *Cowley;* I wrote and wrote, but still I wrote in vain; for after all my Expence of Wit and Pain, a rich unwriting Hand carried the Prize away;[108] with a little Abatement for the last Line: And without being a Witch or any Kin to one, I can dive into that Secret. I well remember that long ago, you promised him a handsome Legacy; which I never did, or had in my Power to do. Nay, I begin to suspect that you were the Impostor, that envying *Delia*'s Glory, went to ask for the private Answer: **[middle column]** for I can assure both you and 'Squire *Hooker, Delia* neither went, nor sent after

---

107 See *Aspasia* on the Dutch and French, *WM*, No. 132 (June 28, 1735). Chapone, as well as Richardson, was probably influenced by Mrs. Delany's stereotypes of foreign behavioral traits.

108 "I like a Fool, did thee Obey,
  I wrote, and wrote, but still I wrote in vain,
  For after all my' expense of Wit and Pain,
  A rich, unwriting Hand, carry'd the Prize away." (page eight)

  Abraham Cowley (1618-1667), "Ode Upon Occasion of a Copy of Verses of my Lord Broghills."
    [https://quod.lib.umich.edu/c/eebo/A34834.0001.001/1:3.3?rgn=div2;view=fulltext]

it. Triumph, *Belinda*! As you please! But however, do not dance over the Grave of your Predecessor. A Time may come, when it shall be said, you have writ for Fame, Self-Interest, or some other bye Ends. Poor *Delia* must throw aside her grey-goose Quill; her vain Pleasantry; and no longer seasonable Mirth; take up the Iron Stile, and try, if possible, to write something more becoming her Age and Circumstances. I have since my first Acquaintance with you, begun and finished a very grave Treatise: But being only a Manuscript Answer to a Manuscript Work; I think it unfair to publish it, until the Author thinks fit that his should see the Light, which I hope, by this time, he has so often reviewed, that he has quite demolished it; and condemn'd it to the Place it best deserves. But however, through your Interest with Mr. *Hooker*, I desire the Favour, that he will be upon the Watch; and if any thing should appear in publick concerning Blood-Puddings,[109] that he will give me timely Notice; that I may have the Pride of saying, it was answered almost as soon as published. It cost me three Days writing; but it is so small, that I think one Day in the Press will be sufficient. I have two more upon the Anvil: One that Mr. *Hooker* never thought worth the calling for: And another, but, oh! I fear the Subject is too weighty to be wielded by the weak Head and Hands of a sickly old Woman, though I have long since writ the Title Page; for I an't like your staunch old Authors, that write first, and then consider what Title is properest. I write the Title Page; and then endeavour to bring the Treatise as near as I can to what I promised my courteous Readers. You see that *Delia*, though not actually dead, is within a Hair's-breadth of it; and must conclude with telling *Belinda*, that in spite of all Quarrels, which at such a time, ought to be laid aside,

I am her real Friend and
Humble Servant,

DELIA.

You see I am forced to make use of an Amanuensis. But if you imagine he had any thing else to do than just to copy my Letter, I shall never forgive you.

---

109 "A large sausage made of blood and suet, sometimes with flour or oatmeal. Cf. blood pudding, blutwurst *n*. Traditionally (in the Black Country and Lancashire) the pudding is boiled; elsewhere in the United Kingdom, Ireland, Canada, etc., it is typically served sliced and grilled as part of a cooked breakfast." OED. *Delia* pretends to be upholding her woman's duty as housekeeper by this curiosity about cookbook recipes.

You find I have poured forth all my Learning in this Epistle; and therefore do not deprive me of the Glory; because I believe it will be the last of this Kind.

19. *Weekly Miscellany*, No. CCCLXIV (364). Saturday, December 15, 1739

Letter on the Methodists.

Some of the *Methodists*, since Mr. *Whitfield* (*sic*)[110] left *England*, and particularly Mr. *John Wesley*, continuing his method of Itinerant Preaching, I beg leave, in your *Weekly Miscellany*, to enquire of these Gentlemen, and earnestly to desire, they would plainly and explicitly declare, what those Principles and Motives are, that seem to determine them to persist in this extraordinary Course.

I am very willing to believe, as they were ordained Ministers of the Church of *England,* that there was a Time, when they sincerely desired and prayed for the Peace of it; when they would have trembled at the thoughts of alienating the Affections of the People from their Parochial Clergy, or encouraging Persons to dissent from them—nor can I conceive, that a fond opinion of their own way of Preaching is the only reason, why they intrude themselves into the most populous Parishes of this Kingdom, industriously endeavouring, and by particular Invitations to *Dissenters,* to increase, I hope not by way of Ostentation, the number of their Hearers—but must rather in Charity conclude, that they do indeed believe, that the Souls of Men are in the utmost danger, and cannot be saved by the Gospel of *Christ,* as it is now commonly preached among us; that they have discover'd some extraordinary Defect in our common Divinity, as Mr. *Whitfield* expresses himself; and therefore find themselves under an indispensible necessity to set Men right, and give them a new Direction, in their way to Heaven.

Letter from Belinda.

SIR,

I formerly gave you a short Account of the State of *Wit* in these Parts, and now I send you a Piece of Intelligence that you may think of more use, tho' your Readers, many of them, may not be so well pleased with it. You may possibly

---

110 George Whitefield (1714–70), evangelical priest, left England for Savannah, Georgia, where he carried on John Wesley's mission. He returned in 1739 to preach to mass audiences in the open air. *ODNB*.

remember the Characters of some young Sparks of this Country who made their Addresses to me in the Habit, Behaviour and Language of very pretty Gentlemen, possessed of all modern Accomplishments, and in none more eminent than in a Freedom from the Prejudices of Education and Religious Superstition. They are still in a State of Celibacy, but they have chang'd their condition to so great a degree, that they can hardly be deem'd the same Men. Their former Briskness was as remarkable as their present Gravity and Formality. *Monsieur,* just arrived with great Alacrity from *Paris,* could not be more *debonair* than they were a few Months since; nor *Aminadab,* from *Pensilvania,*[111] more demure in Look, or more stiff in Gestures and Motion, than they now appear. Play-books and Poems (and not the most modest of them, neither) which supplied them with Topicks and Expressions for Conversation, are chang'd into Scripture Phrases, and others which I never met with in all my Reading; a smutty Sonnet, accompanied with a janty[112] Trip, like insipid Poetry turn'd into dull Prose, are transformed in Hymns of their own composing, and sung with most aukward Distortions of Countenance. These, once hopeful Youths, who had taken so much imprudent care to forget their Catechism, are now with equal Industry *dispersing* Catechisms for the use of the Ladies, and are officious to give us such farther Instructions, by word of Mouth, as may let us into the Secrets of *Methodism,* as they now call their Scheme. Would any Mortal alive have believ'd, six Months ago, that two such promising Geniuses, as the young Mr. *Shallows,* would have look'd into such obsolete things as the Bible, or a Church? And yet, so it is, that they are never easy but when they are in the latter, or expounding the former; which they can do off hand, from *Genesis* to the *Revelations,* with great ease and power. In order to make as great a Revolution in the Appearance of some others, as they have made in themselves, they give away their lac'd Cloths and Shirts, with the rest of their Finery, to some tatter'd Beggars, resolving themselves to wear nothing better than the coursest [*sic*] Attire, and to live upon the most ordinary Diet. Pleasure was formerly the Business of their whole Life, but now every degree of it, however regulated by the strictest Laws of Temperance, Chastity and Prudence is utterly inconsistent with the **[next page]** Purity of their Profession. The old 'Squire has lately made his Will and disinherited them both, because they declared that every Gentleman ought to spend no more upon himself than is absolutely necessary for the Support of Life, but to give it all away to to [*sic*] the Poor, in order to reduce Mankind to the State

---

111 Whitefield had a house in Nazareth, Pennsylvania, close to the Moravian settlement of Bethlehem.
112 "Of persons, their manners, etc.: Well-bred; gentlemanly; genteel. *Obsolete.*" *OED.*

of the primitive Christians; if so, quoth the old Gentleman, I had as good dispose of it myself before I die, as let them fool it away after my Death, which they are taking so much pains to hasten. For the furtherance of this great work of Reformation, they have hired a Barn, where they meet about six in the Evening; expound, pray, and sing Psalms 'till towards ten; then they have a Love-Feast (so I think it is termed,) and afterwards confess the State of their Souls, and communicate their Experiences, especially as to Love Affairs. I was much importuned, for once, out of curiosity, to go to this new Assembly, and I believe I should have gone, if *Letitia Giddy* had not told me of some close Questions that were put to her by the eldest of the Mr. *Shallows*, who before his Conversion was well acquainted with our Sex, and still discovers, in spite of his mortified out-side, some inward hankerings towards us. The Neighbourhood, you may imagine, is much alarmed at these strange Doctrines and Proceedings, and diverse Speculations are raised about them. We young Folks (unless it be some queer Creatures) make it matter of merriment. The Children and Servants run gaping and staring after them, as they would do after any other new Sight; but their Masters and Mistresses, whose Business is neglected, are not so well pleased with the Novelty. The stale Virgins, who had out-liv'd all hopes of any changes in their Condition, 'till they shall change this Life for another, seem to conceive some glimmerings of hope, that in this wonderful Revolution of things something may happen to their advantage; and like many other Adventurers, who purchase Tickets in a bad Lottery, are willing to be in the way of Fortune. Your shrewd ones look upon it as an artful Project to carrry on Intrigues, and steal Heiresses; and are as much frighten'd for their Daughters, as the feather'd Parents are for their tender Offspring when they see the threatening Kite falling around them. When the Mr. *Shallows* make their Progress thro' the Streets to the Barn, with a Mob after them singing Psalms, several pretty Misses have been lock'd up, for that Evening, for fear of worse Pangs than those of the New Birth. As romantick as this Narrative may seem, it is a faithful History of Facts that have really happened. But the most incredible part of the Story is still behind. Great indeed are the Changes already related, but much greater are those which I am now going to mention. These Gentlemen have not only laid aside their natural Looks, their former Language, and way of Life, but their natural or acquired Dispositions of Mind. The Voluptuous no longer desires soft Clothing and to fare sumptuously every day, but is fallen in love with Sackcloth[113] and Soup-meagre.[114] The late Man of Gallantry declares openly for

---

113 "As the material of mourning or penitential garb; also (in contrast with 'purple' or 'gold') as the coarsest possible clothing, indicative of extreme poverty or humility." *OED*
114 "Thin soup, made chiefly from vegetables or fish." *OED*

the strictest Chastity, and would not for the world so much as cast a Sheep's Eye after a pretty Girl, or touch her little Finger, if he should chance unwillingly to stumble upon one; tho' just before his Regeneration he would have broke his Neck over Hedge and Ditch at the sight of a Petticoat. Wonderful Luck this! beyond what every body can meet with! Since your Lecture upon Habits, I have been trying with my utmost Resolution, to get the better of Snuff, but I have been able to gain but few Pinches in a day. Possibly you may be making as slow a progress in Tobacco. They, without any difficulty, have got the Dominion over themselves. But the manner of this great Change is as extraordinary as the Change itself. It is wrought instantaneously, without their concurrence, by a Divine Operation; nay, what is till more strange, good Works and virtuous Dispositions are so far from recommending them in the Blessing of this total Alteration of their Nature, **[middle column]** that the more wicked the Object, the better qualified for this divine Operation. They have made me a charitable Visit, in hopes of converting me, and strongly urg'd the great Advantages of Wickedness as a Qualification for the *Spirit:* from whence I could not help concluding that they wanted to qualify me for it, and desired them to make their Bows, if they did not think it sinful, and seek out for Persons more fit for their purpose.

I am,
Your unregenerated,
But sincere Friend,

Northamptonshire.   BELINDA.

My Humble Service to *Delia.*

20. Weekly Miscellany, No. CCCCXXI (421). Saturday, January 17, 1740

Mr. HOOKER.

In my last, bearing date I know not when, I gave you to understand that I did not purpose to write to you any more; which Resolution has been very much strengthen'd by some unfortunate Circumstances that have happen'd since. But however averse, or unqualified I may be to appear again in Print, I am obliged in Vindication of my own Honour and Modesty to do it. You must know, Sir, that since my coming to Town this Winter, having lost my gay Taste for Plays, Novels, and all such kind of Amusements, I am turn'd a most notable Politician; and by way of Qualification, as well as Entertainment in my Retirement, I got a Sight of all the political Journalists, that I might take one of them in constantly. The *Craftsman* I had several Objections against. Tho' I never admired a Coxcomb, or a Fop, I never could bear a heavy, slovenly Fellow. I ask the Gentleman's Pardon for making so free with him, but he is as dull and tedious in his Discourses, and as dirty in his Dress, as the Parson of our Parish. I was afraid of taking up his Paper for fear of fouling my Fingers. It is scarce fit to wrap up brown Sugar in. *Common Sense*,[115] I own, makes a good spruce Figure, and is tolerably smart sometimes; but, then, his Family were never much in Favour with our Sex, and I should have been more singular than I ever care to be if I had declared in Favour of him. I had now no Choice let, but I was forced to take up *Captain Hercules Vinegar*,[116] tho' I was somewhat prejudiced against him by a former *Miscellany*, which hinted as if he were not so well affected to the *Clergy* as I could wish. What I thought of his Lucubrations, or how I lik'd his *Rumours, Advices,* and *Puffs*, I shall not mention. I am going to disband him, and let him, if he can, fight his Way thro' all Opposition. I shall do him no farther Injury than is necessary towards doing my self Justice, by letting your Readers know why I have discarded him. In short, he has lately put on *Pinners* and a *Petticoat*; and any one might easily guess what a staring, frightful Figure, the *Champion* of *England*, the *Hercules* of the Age, must make in *female Attire*, and what a Disgrace he has done us by such a monstrous Representation. But not content with doing Dishonour to our Persons, he has brought Infamy upon our Characters, by talking as filthily as he looks. A Bawd in Breeches, canting about Regeneration and the Pangs of the New Birth, or a Debauchee in a Gown and Cassock, preaching up Repentance and a pious Life, could not act a more unnatural Part, or act it more awkwardly. As a *Woman* I resent it, in Honour of my Sex. But he has offended and injured me in a particular Manner, by assuming my *Name* too; the more because, as I have taken in his Paper, his nasty Performance will be the more likely to pass for mine, by those who are not acquainted with me, and give the envious Prude an Occasion for Scandal, and the wanton Flirt an Example to justify her immodest Freedoms. Besides, tho' I was not in a Humour to continue a Correspondence with you, I would not have 'Squire *Hooker* think *Belinda* would discard him for any other Champion. You are engaged in a nobler Cause, and better deserve **[middle column]** the Title than any of your Brethren, as well a better answer it. As it is the Business of [a] *Champion* to engage the *Enemies* of his Country, and of an *Hercules* to rid the World of *Monsters*, you attack our *greatest* Enemies and the *greatest* Monsters that can infest and ravage a Nation, the Enemies of *Religion* and *Virtue*; But *Captain Vinegar* attacks the Honour of the *Fair*, whom all true Warriors have

---

115 Henry Fielding contributed anonymous essays to both the periodicals *The Craftsman* and *Common Sense*. *ODNB*.

116 See Introduction, footnote 12. Alludes to *The Champion* (January 1, 1739–40).

thought themselves obliged to defend, and makes himself a Greater Monster than the GREAT *Hercules* himself ever subdued. Be pleased, therefore, to let the *Captain* know that it was below his Character to put a Parcel of little smutty Stuff into the Mouth of a Lady, and a Piece of Injustice to affix to it the Name of your much injur'd

BELINDA.

P. S. Let any one look into my Letters published in the two Volumes of the *Miscellanies,* and see whether I have been used to write in such an impudent Manner.

From my Lodging in Westminster,[117]
    Jan. 10. 1741.

Having had a Present made me of a small Volume of *Familiar Letters,* written on the most usual Subjects in Common Life, not yet published, I cannot help anticipating the Pleasure it will give when it appears, by taking from it the following Letter, which I hope the Writer will not take amiss.[118]

---

117 As printer for the House of Commons Richardson spent considerable time in Westminster.
118 It is probably no coincidence that this puff for Richardson's forthcoming *Familiar Letters* occurs below *Belinda*'s letter.

CONCLUSION: RICHARDSON'S PRESS AND WOMEN'S ENTRY INTO PUBLIC LIFE

During the first two decades of his career, Richardson's role as printer was hardly limited to setting the type for the periodicals that were issued from his shop. Perhaps the most glaring evidence of his intervention in producing text is the fact that both *The True Briton* and *The Weekly Miscellany* just happen to have letters supposedly from women who protested the legal restraints against their participation in the public sphere. Neither the Duke of Wharton, the owner of *The True Briton*, nor William Webster, the desperately impecunious producer of *The Weekly Miscellany*, launched their journals with the objective of advancing radical views about political equality for women. But almost inadvertently, this middle-aged, rotund printer at Salisbury Court was quietly feminizing journalism.

As an outlier in what was perceived to be a corrupt, predatory political world, Richardson readily assumed a female role as victim and the subversive strategy of passive resistance. The Non-juror *TB* females voiced dilemmas over being required to swear oaths of loyalty to a government that their consciences could not support:

> For my own Part, I am under the greatest Anxiety, having a small Fortune, and a numerous Family: If I take the Oaths required of me, I swear to Things I have no certain Knowledge of; and the Author of *The Whole Duty of Man* tells me (Page the 100) "If I swear to the Truth of that whereof I am only doubtful, though the Thing should happen to be true; yet it brings upon me the Guilt of Perjury; for I swear at a Venture, and the Thing might, for ought I know, be as well false as true;

whereas I ought never to swear any thing the Truth of which I do not certainly know."[1]

This oath of obedience to government authority also includes the dilemma concerning marriage vows and the legal dominance of husbands over wives, as Sarah Chapone argues:

> In Short, either Wives can judge how far, and in what Instances an Husband is to be obeyed, or they cannot: If they are so undiscerning as not to be able to perceive the essential Difference between obeying their Husbands in the Lord, and in the direct Opposition to and Defiance of him; then let their blind Obedience to their Husbands excuse them in the Case of Treason as well as it does in other Cases: But if they cannot plead this Darkness of the Understanding, why are they treated like Children or Idiots? I can assign but one Reason for these Inconsistencies, namely, that it is for the Interest of the Community as a Body Politick, that Wives should be punish'd as free Agents for Treason, but that, in Respect to the private Royalties of Husbands, in other Cases they are not expected to judge of Right and of Wrong; 'tis sufficient for them, if their Actions confess they accede to the Jurisdiction of their Husbands.[2]

In *WM*, Richardson evolved from giving single female impersonations undergoing crises of conscience to a domestic arrangement where the feminist *Belinda* is under the care of a morally stern aunt and her religious mentor. We are not told where her parents have gone, but their omission leaves more freedom for her ironic distancing from the surrogate authority. It is relatively harmless to criticize an aunt than a mother or father. Given Richardson's lifelong insistence on the child's obedience to her parents, his plots often remove them from the scenes of presenting a budding feminist heroine like *Pamela* or *Harriet Byron*. There the isolated protagonist must fend for herself without a guardian angel nearby. By contrast, the all-too-obtrusive presence of the *Harlowe* family is programmed for the tragic resistance of *Clarissa* in what is mistakenly believed to be her "treasonous" elopement with a libertine and her father's subsequent curse.

Conversation in masquerade was the mode of communication in a repressive world where women were especially fearful of censorship and opprobrium. But quite unrelated from this feminist strategy, Richardson also uses

---

[1] *The True Briton*, No. 45 (November 4. 1723).
[2] *Hardships*, p. 36.

this device to give hints to the editor, Webster. Aside from the alleged purpose of adding comedic voices to *WM*, *Belinda* often insinuates Richardson's role as a financial supporter of Webster's struggling periodical as well as blunt criticism of this periodical's "dullness." Anonymity gives freedom to the writer to divulge secret intentions and purposes. *Belinda* unleashes a satiric impulse emulating Swift that Richardson seldom reveals in his "histories" except, of course, in such scenes rendering class differences as in *Pamela* among the gentry or *Clarissa* at Mrs. Sinclair's.

> But Mr. *Blunt* put an End to the Debate, with a short but pithy Speech: "As to the *Protestant Interest*, it is safe enough. Let the *Clergy*, by *Celibacy*, be ever so much *detach'd* from the common Interest of the Nation, if they have neither *Money* nor *Power*, they can do neither Hurt nor Good. As to our *Wives* and *Daughters* they can be in no great Danger from them, while we take Care to make them so *odious* and *contemptible*. But *here* lies the great Point of all: We must make them all as *poor* as we can, that they may be *inconsiderable*, and therefore let the Rogues *marry* and *get Children* as fast as they will; this must make them still *poorer*, and answer our Intention better than the *Quakers Bill*."

Obviously frustrated with the public's demand for irony as opposed to the neutral tone of theological disputations, *Hooker* himself ruefully acknowledged this aspect of *Belinda*'s banter.[3]

Elsewhere, Richardson seems to deliberately avoid irony for the sake of a pithy aphorism. His *Collection of Moral Sentiments* reveals little of the witty turns of La Rochefoucauld's *Maxims*, with their obvious bias against received platitudes. Instead, when "writing to the moment," Richardson focused on the individual "female" soul's tormented dialogue to reach the sentiment: "'tis not in our power to offend."

> WHAT have we done? Or, What can we do? That we should have this Hardship laid upon our Sex? A Sex so helpless and defenceless, that, had we the Inclination (as far be it from us) 'tis not in our Power to offend. We cannot take up Arms ourselves, and we have no Influence over the Men 'tis plain, if we had, this Act had never pass'd: Or if we

---

3 "But must no Man undertake the Cause of God and his Country, against the common Enemies of both, unless he is blessed with the superior Genius of a *Swift*, a *Pope*, or an *Arbuthnot*?" *WM*, No. 27 (June 16, 1733).

would give our whole Estates to assist a Rebellion, our Sex would hardly be trusted with the Secret. *TB,* No. 45 (November 4, 1723)

Thus, from his earliest years as a printer throughout his career as a novelist, it is the "helpless and defenceless" female that is the *leitmotif* of his narrative discourse.

As a means of contrasting the ideal union of equal minds and hearts to the more likely situation where the woman enjoys imaginary power during courtship before succumbing to servitude after marriage, Harriet Byron tries to rally her future sister-in-law, Charlotte, who is in a quandary about her upcoming marriage to Lord G.

> Do you think I can be happy with Lord G.?
>
> I am sure you may, if it be not your own fault.
>
> That's the thing: I may perhaps bear with the man; but I cannot honour him.
>
> Then don't *vow* to honour him. Don't meet him at the altar.
>
> Yet I must. But I believe I think too much: And consideration is no friend to wedlock.—Would to heaven that the same hour that my hand and Lord G.'s were joined, yours and my brother's were also united![4]

Once again, we have the woman agonizing over taking vows that her conscience cannot accept. Charlotte's confession: "But I believe I think too much: And consideration [meditation][5] is no friend to wedlock" seems to be a surrender to the woman's "defencelessness." Never challenged, of course, not even by Mary Astell and Sarah Chapone, is the Pauline doctrine of the Fall and woman's resultant subordination.

So no, this little volume of female voices crying out for freedom still leaves us adrift from real legal equality between the sexes, despite the historical opening up of the press to allow their entry into the public sphere. Even today, the struggle continues. Nevertheless, in his lifelong work on behalf of female literacy, as I hope this collection indicates, Richardson surely deserves a place next to his Gloucestershire friend as a "champion of her sex."

---

4 *Grandison,* 3rd ed. (1754), Vol. 4, Letter XI, pp. 89–90 [Thursday morning, April 6].
5 "consideration, n.
   The keeping of a subject before the mind; attentive thought, reflection, meditation." *OED.*

BIBLIOGRAPHY

Primary Sources

Abbreviations:

FM: Forster Collection, Victoria and Albert Museum.
ODNB: *Oxford Dictionary of National Biograhy.*
OED: *Oxford English Dictionary.*

The True Briton. Written by Philip, Duke of Wharton. In Two Volumes (London, [1723]). Printed by Richardson. Maslen 834 & 835.
The Weekly Miscellany copied from Gale Primary Sources: Seventeenth and Eighteenth Century Burney Newspapers Collection accessed through the University of Illinois Library.

Richardson, Samuel:

Carroll, John, ed. *Selected Letters of Samuel Richardson* (Oxford: Clarendon, 1964).
Gerard, Christine, ed. *The Cambridge Edition of the Correspondence of Samuel Richardson: Correspondence with Aaron Hill and the Hill Family*. The Cambridge Edition of the Correspondence of Samuel Richardson (Cambridge: Cambridge University Press, 2013).
Dussinger, John A. *The Cambridge Edition of the Correspondence of Samuel Richardson: Correspondence with George Cheyne and Thomas Edwards*, ed. David E. Shuttleton and John A. Dussinger (Cambridge: Cambridge University Press, 2013).
Dussinger, John A. *The Cambridge Edition of the Correspondence of Samuel Richardson: Correspondence with Sarah Wescomb, Frances Grainger, and Laetitia Pilkington*, ed. John A. Dussinger (Cambridge: Cambridge University Press, 2015).
Sabor, Peter. *The Cambridge Edition of the Correspondence of Samuel Richardson: Correspondence with Lady Bradshaigh and Lady Echlin*. 3 vols (Cambridge: Cambridge University Press, 2016).
Familiar Letters: Letters written to and for particular friends: on the most important occasions. Directing not only the requisite style and forms to be observed in writing familiar letters; but how to think and act justly and prudently, in the common concerns of human life. 4th edn. (1750). Chadwyck-Healey database of *Eighteenth-Century Fiction* (new platform *ProQuest*) accessed through the University of Illinois Library.
Rivero, Albert J., ed. *Pamela: Or, Virtue Rewarded*. The Cambridge Edition of the Works of Samuel Richardson (Cambridge: Cambridge University Press, 2011).

Rivero, Albert J., ed. *Pamela in her Exalted Condition*. The Cambridge Edition of the Works of Samuel Richardson (Cambridge: Cambridge University Press, 2012).

* * * *

Besides depending on the Chadwyck-Healy database of *Eighteenth-Century Fiction*, new platform *ProQuest*, I have had the benefit of my own collection of Richardson's three *Histories*:

> [Richardson, Samuel]. *Pamela. Or, Virtue Rewarded. In a Series of Familiar Letters from a Beautiful Young Damsel to her Parents: and afterwards, In her Exalted Condition, Between Her, and Persons of Figure and Quality, Upon the Most Important and Entertaining Subjects, In Genteel Life. In Four Volumes. Publish'd in order to cultivate the Principles of Virtue and Religion in the Minds of the Youth of Both Sexes. The Sixth Edition, Corrected. And Embellish'd with Copper Plates, Design'd and Engrav'd by Mr. Hayman, and Mr. Gravelot.* London: Printed for S. Richardson; And sold by J. Osborn, in Pater-noster Row; and John Rivington, in St. Paul's Church-yard. M.DCCXLII.

The first two volumes are corrected 6th editions; the third and fourth are corrected 3rd editions. "The third edition of Vols. III and IV was published with the sixth edition of Vols. I and II in May, 1742. The first edition of Vols. III and IV had been published as a sequel in two volumes in December, 1741. The second edition of Vols. III and IV was not, I believe, published until after the third edition of these volumes (see no. 16). Consequently, this was the first occasion on which the novel was published as a work in four volumes." Sale (1936), p. 21.

> [Richardson, Samuel]. *Clarissa. Or, The History of Young Lady: Comprehending the most Important Concerns of Private Life. And particularly shewing, The Distresses that may attend the Misconduct both of Parents and Children, in Relation to Marriage.* Published by the Editor of Pamela. London: Printed for S. Richardson; And Sold by A. Millar, J. and Ja. Rivington, John Osborn, and by J. Leake at Bath, 1748.

First edition, 7 volumes, 12mo, apart from slight occasional spotting or soiling and a few insignificant marginal tears (neatly mended without loss) a very good copy; folding leaf of engraved music in Vol. II, Vols. III and IV in first state (i.e., with the Preface in IV), all the usual cancels (C2, C11, E2 in Vol. III, M5 in Vol. V, and E10 in Vol. VI), the erratum on p. 149 in Vol. IV corrected, L12 in Vol. VI excised as usual with the text continuing on M1 rather than on a cancellans; full green crushed levant, gilt, all edges gilt, by Riviere. Rothschild 1749, Sale (1936), p. 32, Black 6911.

> [Richardson, Samuel]. *Clarissa. Or, The History of Young Lady: Comprehending the most Important Concerns of Private Life. In Eight Volumes. To Each of which is added A TABLE OF CONTENTS. The Third Edition. In which Many Passages and some Letters are restored from the Original Manuscripts. And to which is added, An ample Collection of such of the Moral and Instructive Sentiments interspersed throughout the Work, as may be presumed to be of general Use and Service.* London: Printed for S. Richardson; And Sold by John Osborn, in Pater-noster Row; By Andrew Millar, over-against Catharine-street in the Strand; By J. and Ja. Rivington, in St. Paul's Church-yard; And by J. Leake at Bath, 1751, 8 vols., 12⁰. (Published simultaneously with the fourth edition, 7 vols., 8⁰).

BIBLIOGRAPHY

[Richardson, Samuel]. *The History of Sir Charles Grandison. In a Series of Letters Published from the Originals, By the Editor of* PAMELA *and* CLARISSA. In Seven Volumes. The Third Edition. London: Printed for S. Richardson; And sold by C. Hitch and L. Hawes, in Pater-noster Row; By J. and J. Rivington, in St. Paul's Church-Yard; By Andrew Millar, in the Strand; By R. and J. Dodsley, in Pall-Mall; And by J. Leake, at Bath. 1754.

* * * *

[Chapone, Sarah Kirkham]:

Glover, Susan Paterson, ed. *The Hardships of the English Laws in Relation to Wives by Sarah Chapone* (London and New York: Routledge, 2018).

[Chapone, Sarah Kirkham]. *Remarks on Mrs. Muilman's Letter to the Right Honourable the Earl of Chesterfield. In a Letter to Mrs. Muilman. By a Lady.* 2nd ed. (1750). Printed by Richardson. Maslen 130.

Delany, Mary (1700–1788). *The Autobiography and Correspondence of Mary Granville, Mrs Delany*, ed. Lady Llanover. 1st ser., 3 vols. (1861), Vol. I, pp. 15–16.

Delany, Patrick. *Revelation Examined with Candour. Or, a fair enquiry into the sense and use of the several revelations expressly declared, or sufficiently implied, To be given to Mankind from the Creation, as they are found in the Bible. By a profess'd friend to an honest freedom of thought in religious enquiries. [...] Containing Dissertations on the following Subjects; viz. I. Of the Forbidden Fruit. II. Of the Knowledge of the Brute World conveyed to Adam. III. Of his Knowledge of Marriage. IV. Of the Skill of Language infused into Adam. V. Of the Revelations immediately following the Fall. VI. Of the Mosaic Account of the Fall. Vii. Of Sacrifices. Viii. Of the Corruptions of Mankind, which caused the Deluge. IX. Of the natural Causes made use of by God to flood the Earth. X. Of the Ends of Divine Wisdom answered by the Deluge. XI. Of the Objections to the Mosaic Account of the Deluge. XII. Of the Concurrence of all Antiquity with the Mosaic Account of the Flood. XIII. Of other Testimonies relating to the Deluge. XIV. Of the Difficulties relating to Noah's Ark* (1732). Maslen 228–235.

Delany, Patrick. *The Present State of Learning, Religion, and Infidelity in Great-Britain. Wherein The Causes of the present Degeneracy of Taste, and Increase of Infidelity, are inquir'd into, and accounted for. Publish'd by a sincere friend to the cause of religion and virtue, With a View To awaken the Secure, to stimulate the Lukewarm, to chastise the Profligate, and to animate the Professors of Christianity, to do their Duty, maugre all Discouragements, &c. Written by the Reverend Dr. Delany* (1732). Not in Maslen but printed by Richardson, who is probably Delany's declared "sincere friend."

Dennis, John. *Remarks on Mr. Pope's* RAPE OF THE LOCK (1728). Maslen, p. 239.

Duncombe, John. *The Feminiad* (London, 1754).

[Fielding, Henry]. *The Champion* (January 1, 1739–40).

Hill, Aaron. *The Works of the Late Aaron Hill*, 2nd ed. (London, 1754).

Hill, Aaron. *The Prompter* (11734–36). Maslen, p. 30.

[Newton, Richard]. *Pluralities Indefensible. A Treatise Humbly Offered to the Consideration of the Parliament of Great Britain. By a Presbyter of the Church of England* (1743). Maslen, pp. 537–538.

Webster, William. *A Plain Narrative of Facts, or, the Author's Case Fairly and Candidly Stated, By Way of Appeal to the Publick* (1758).

Secondary Sources

Broad, Jaqueline. *The Philosophy of Mary Astell: An Early Modern Theory of Virtue* (Oxford: Oxford University Press, 2015).

Curran, Louise. *Samuel Richardson and the Art of Letter-Writing* (Cambridge: Cambridge University Press, 2016).

Dussinger, John A. "Samuel Richardson's 'Elegant Disquisitions': Anonymous Writing in the *True Briton* and Other Journals?" *Studies in Bibliography*, 53 (2000), 195–226.

Dussinger, John A. and Mary Astell. *Some Reflections upon Marriage* (1700), ed. John A. Dussinger, with introduction, Women in Print ebooks (Urbana: University of Illinois Press, 2015).

Dussinger, John A. "'Stealing in the Great Doctrines of Christianity': Samuel Richardson as Journalist," *Eighteenth-Century Fiction*, 15 (April–July 2003), 451–506.

Dussinger, John A. "Fabrications from Samuel Richardson's Press," *Papers for the Bibliographical Society*, 100:2 (2006), 259–79.

Dussinger, John A. "Another Anonymous Compilation from Samuel Richardson's Press: *A Select Manual of Devotions for Sick Persons* (1733)," *Papers for the Bibliographical Society of America*, 102:3 (2008), 363–85.

Dussinger, John A. "The Oxford Methodists (1733; 1738): The Purloined Letter of John Wesley at Samuel Richardson's Press," Chapter Two, *Theology and Literature in the Age of Johnson: Resisting Secularism*, ed. Melvyn New and Gerard Reedy (Newark: University of Delaware Press, 2012), 27–48.

Dussinger, John A. "Mary Astell's Revisions of *Some Reflections upon Marriage* (1730)," *Papers for the Bibliographical Society of America*, 107:1 (2013), 49–79.

Eaves, T. C. Duncan and Ben D. Kimpel, *Samuel Richardson: A Biography* (Oxford: Clarendon, 1971).

Harris, Michael. *London Newspapers in the Age of Walpole: A Study of the Origins of the Modern English Press* (Rutherford, Madison, Teaneck: Fairleigh Dickinson University Press; London and Toronto: Associate University Presses, 1987).

Maruca, Lisa. *The Work of Print: Authorship and the English Text Trades, 1660–1760* (Seattle and London: University of Washington Press, 2007).

Maslen, Keith. *Samuel Richardson of London Printer A Study of his Printing Based on Ornament Use and Business Accounts* (Dunedin: University of Otago Press [Department of English], 2001).

Melville, Lewis. *The Life and Writings of Philip Duke of Wharton* (London: John Lane the Bodley Head; New York: John Lane Company Toronto Bell & Cockburn, 1913). https://archive.org/details/lifewritingsofph00benjuoft/page/n7/mode/2up?view =theater

Mullan, John. *Anonymity: A Secret History of English Literature* (Princeton: Princeton University Press, 2007).

Pearce, Edward. *The Great Man: Sir Robert Walpole: Scoundrel, Genius and Britain's First Prime Minister* (London: Random House, 2007).

Sale Jr., William M. *Samuel Richardson: Master Printer* (Ithaca: Cornell University Press, 1950).

Slatterly, William C., ed. *The Richardson-Stinstra Correspondence and Stinstra's Prefaces to Clarissa* (Carbondale and Edwardsville: Southern Illinois University Press, 1969).

Sowall, Alice and Penny A. Weiss, eds. *Feminist Interpretations of Mary Astell* (University Park: Penn State, 2016).

Vallance, Edward. "Women, Politics and the 1723 Oaths of Allegiance to George I," *The Historical Journal*, 29:4 (2016), 975–999.

Vulliamy, C. E. *Aspasia: The Life and Letters of Mary Granville, Mrs. Delany (1700–1788)* (London: Geoffrey Bles, 1935).

Weber, Harold. *Memory, Print, and Gender in England, 1653–1759*. Early Modern Cultural Studies, 1500–1700 (New York: Palgrave Macmillan, 2008).

* * *

As a supplement to my attributions, whenever stylistic peculiarities appear I offer the results of comparative word and phrase searches in the Chadwyck-Healey database *Eighteenth-Century Fiction*, new platform *ProQuest*, which reproduces the full texts of 96 works of British fiction published between 1700 and 1780. In *TB*, No. 34, two words seem to be favorite terms in Richardson's prose. Thus the word "blunderer" in the plural appears only in *Clarissa*—once in the first edition and twice in the third. The word "vociferated" appears twice in each edition of *Clarissa* and twice in one other novel (Henry Brook's *Fool of Quality*). The brief references here are therefore given as follows:

"Blunderers" 3/3

"vociferated" 2/4

I do not claim these comparisons as proof of attribution. But they do indicate the relative frequency of words or phrases associated with the fiction by Richardson included in this database and thus some degree, no matter how tentative, of probability about the source.

INDEX

Addison, Joseph 15
Allestree, Richard 18, 22; *Whole Duty of Man, The* 18, 22, 129
Astell, Mary 35–36, 38, 132
Atterbury, Francis 2–3, 5, 8, 10
Atwood, Margaret 41

Bellarmine, Robert 13–14
"Bloody Assizes" 2–3

Carter, Mary 38, 76
Cave, Edward 1
Cervantes Saavedra, Miguel de 119; *Don Quixote* 119
Champion, "Championess" 16–17, 33–34, 42, 89, 126–27, 132
Chapone, Sarah (née Kirkham) 25, 35–45, 72, 75–76, 78, 80–81, 86, 89, 97–99; *Hardships of the English Laws regarding Wives, The* 25, 36–40, 59, 75–77, 96, 98, 106, 114, 130
Chubb, Thomas 63
Clarissa 2, 10, 26–27, 32, 35, 38, 76, 84, 101, 103, 130–31
Collier, Jeremy 59
Congreve, William 25; *Old Batchelor, The* 25
Conscience 4, 8, 10, 13, 18–24, 60–61, 86–89, 98, 129–30, 132
Courtship 35–36, 68–70, 74, 86–89, 102, 132
Cowley, Abraham 120

Delany, May (née Granville) 37, 60, 120
Delany, Patrick 37–38, 59
Dennis, John 32
Duncombe, John 40; *Feminiad, The* 40

Edwards, Thomas 40, 41

Familiar Letters 35–36, 54, 127
Fielding, Henry 19, 33–34, 126

Gibson, Edmund, Lord Bishop of London 4–5
Gordon, Thomas 63–64
Grandison, History of Sir Charles 29, 35, 41–42, 54, 60, 99, 100, 132
"grave" 31, 34, 48, 52, 57, 59, 69, 81, 85–86, 94, 98–100, 114
Grimston, William 69

Henley, John 82
Hill, Aaron 43–44, 69
Hobbes, Thomas 59

Jacobite Rebellion of 1721–1722 2

Kennet, White 7

Le Grand, Anthony 102
Lemnos, island of, husbands massacred by wives 7
Livings, pluralities 30, 35, 64
Locke, John 55

Mapp, Sarah (née Wallin) 82
Maslen, Keith 2, 29–32, 37, 44, 55, 59, 64, 100, 102, 133, 135
Masquerade 4–5, 25–26, 32, 43, 76, 83, 130
Methodist 1, 31, 36–38, 122
Monmouth, Duke of 2

Newton, Richard 30; *Pluralities Indefensible,* 30
Nichols, John 1

Oaths 5–8, 10, 13, 17–25, 116, 129; "Swear" 6, 9, 11–13, 18–19, 22–24, 57–68, 73, 96, 129–30

Oaths of Allegiance 6
Onslow, Arthur 13, 65
Overbury, Thomas 59
Ovid 17; *Ars Amatoria* 17

Pamela 14, 30–34, 36, 43–45, 54–55, 62–63, 83, 91, 102, 130–31
Papirius 11; Gellius, Aulus, *Attic Nights, The* 11; Macrobius, Ambrosius Aurelius Theodosius, *Saturnalia* 11
Plutarch 3; *Political Precepts* 3
Pope, Alexander 16, 31–32, 50, 55, 101, 131

Quaker Act of 1721, 13, 19, 66

"Religion is a cheerful Thing" 31–32, 34, 103
Richardson, Samuel: correspondence with Sarah Chapone 37; correspondence with Sarah Wescomb 55; correspondence with Thomas Edwards 40–41
Riot Act of 1715 8

Savile, George, Marquess of Halifax 70, 77
Seneca, Lucius Annaeus 102
Shaftesbury, first Earl of 2
South Sea Bubble of 1720, 2–3, 9
Stinstra, Johannes 2
Swift, Jonathan 50, 66, 79, 131

Toland, John 9

Vallance, Edward 5, 10, 20

Wake, William 22
Walpole, Robert 2–3, 29
Webster, William 4, 29–32, 34–35, 38, 40, 42, 53, 62, 75–76, 78, 98–99, 111, 113, 129, 131
Wesley, John 37–38, 122
Wharton, Philip, Duke of, 2–3, 5, 11–14, 29, 129
Whitefield, George 122–23
"Woful experience of your printer," 14, 32
Woolaston, William 59

Milton Keynes UK
Ingram Content Group UK Ltd.
UKHW011959110224
437587UK00003B/66